GOD'S FINANCIAL PLAN

YOUR PATH TO DEBT FREEDOM AND BIBLICAL ABUNDANCE

ROD NICHOLS

Unless otherwise identified Scripture quotations are from the New International Version®, NIV® Copyright ©1973, 1978, 1984, 2011 by Biblica, Inc.® Used by permission.

Scripture quotations marked NLT are from the New Living Translation, copyright © 1996, 2004, 2015 by Tyndale House Foundation. Used by permission of Tyndale House Publishers, Inc., Carol Stream, Illinois 60188.

Scripture quotations marked NASB are from the New American Standard Bible, Copyright © 1960, 1962, 1963, 1968, 1971, 1972, 1973, 1975, 1977, 1995, 2020 by The Lockman Foundation.

Scripture quotations marked KJV are from the King James Version. Public domain.

Scripture quotations marked NKJV are from the New King James Version®. Copyright © 1982 by Thomas Nelson. Used by permission.

Publishing Coordinator – Sharon Kizziah-Holmes

Paperback-Press
an imprint of A & S Publishing
Paperback Press, LLC.

ISBN -13: 978-1-956806-74-8

ACKNOWLEDGMENTS

First, I want to acknowledge God for His financial plan and for the Holy Spirit who guided us down the road and was patient with me, as I went off on my own.

This road, to discovering God's financial plan, has been a rocky one and so I want to thank Karen, my wife and the love of my life, for walking down the road with me. If not for her, I probably would have fallen off the financial cliff. Thanks, baby!

I also want to thank Sharon Kizziah-Holmes at Paperback Press for her work in the professional layout of the book and Jaycee DeLorenzo for the amazing cover.

TABLE OF CONTENTS

INTRODUCTION

The world has its financial plan; you've seen the bumper stickers – "He who dies with the most toys wins." In the eyes of the world, those people with the greatest amount of money and material things are the real winners. The problem with that is that material things are only temporary, while spiritual things are eternal. The key here is that we are transcending two realms: the physical and the spiritual. God wants us to be prosperous in both realms and in all parts of our lives.

This book contains the principles of God's financial plan. It will teach you how to be prosperous both here on earth and in heaven. As born-again believers in Jesus Christ, we operate in both realms simultaneously. We have flesh and blood bodies that function in this earthly realm, and we have a spirit that is connected to God through the Holy Spirit and operates in the heavenly realm. In fact, in Ephesians 2:6, it says, *"And God raised us up with Christ and seated us with him in the heavenly realms in Christ Jesus."* Even as we live here on earth, we are also seated at the right hand of Father God, in Christ. It is important for our financial wellbeing and the growth of the church, that we understand how to operate in both realms.

This material was developed after years of prayer and petition. The principles were first taught in a class in the spring of 2001. The fruit, from that class and many that followed, was amazing. Students put these simple principles into action and spiritual and financial blessings were abundantly evident in all of their lives. You will encounter many of these amazing stories throughout the book.

One such story is how Karen, my wife, and I used this wisdom to eliminate $120,000 worth of consumer debt in just 5 years. We had many people counseling us to declare bankruptcy and get a fresh start, but we knew that wasn't the right way to handle the debt. In prayer, we received confirmation and began to seek God for wisdom. I will share that wisdom later in the book.

The world wants you to believe that their way is the best – climbing the corporate ladder, while disregarding your family; get rich quick schemes that require no work, and you make millions; internet selling programs; the lottery and gambling; real estate investing; and so on. While it is important to have financial vehicles, if you seek God first, He will open those doors for you.

A great example of this was shared by my friend, David Herzog, in his book *Secrets of the Glory* (you can purchase this amazing book at www.thegloryzone.org). David shared that he was just learning how to operate in both realms and in 2003 God told him to buy a house. It's important to understand that David and his wife, Stephanie, had been missionaries in France for many years and had no money. When David inquired of the Lord about where the money would come from, the Lord referred him to Proverbs 13:22, "*the wealth of the wicked is reserved for the righteous*". David asked the Lord where this wealth was, and His response was that the money was in the bank. David expounded on the story, but I will give the short version. Ultimately, David went to the bank, completed an application, and was approved for a zero-down loan. He then bought a condominium with no money out of his pocket. Two years later, they sold the condo for double what they paid. We have a similar story, that I will share later in the book. That's operating in both realms at the same time. It's God's financial plan.

God wants His children to be the most prosperous people on earth. Unfortunately, many Christians have been taught that prosperity is sinful. Scriptures such as Matthew 19:24, "*Again I tell you, it is easier for a camel to go through the eye of a needle than for a rich man to enter the kingdom of God*" and others, have been used to misinform and paralyze Christians. This is all part of satan's plan to bind the children of God and slow the growth of the Kingdom. After all, who is going to finance the spreading of the gospel, if Christians don't? Who is going to pay for the Bibles? Who is going to send out the missionaries? Who is going to build the orphanages and feed the poor? The world sure isn't, so it's up to us to discover how to operate in God's financial plan.

In Jeremiah 29:11, God makes it clear that His plan is to prosper His children. He is speaking to the Israelites at the time, but we, as born-again believers, are grafted into God's family, so it also applies to us today. Here is what God says, "'*For I know the plans I have for you,' declares the* LORD, '*plans to prosper you and not to harm you, plans to give you hope and a future.*'" Now, you may immediately bristle at the idea of prosperity, because many have misused the word, so let's take a look at the original language, Hebrew, to see what God was really saying.

The Hebrew word that is translated as prosperity in the NIV is the word *Shalowm*. We hear this word quite often and it is typically referencing peace, which is one of the definitions of the word. However, some other definitions are completeness (lacking nothing), welfare (doing well), contentment (happy with life), and prosperity. So, if we look at all of those definitions, then *Shalowm* or prosperity, as we are using it here in this book, would mean lacking nothing that is needed, resulting in complete welfare and contentment in all parts of life. In short, you are not lacking in your health, relationships, career, and finances. When God says He wants to prosper you, He wants you complete, not lacking anything. In the balance of this book, we are going to talk about the financial aspect of prosperity, but true prosperity applies to your entire life. Seek God first and He will prosper you.

In the following pages, you will learn about the proper mindset and beliefs, financial stewardship, how to partner with God, the principles of sowing and reaping, why it's important to tithe and give beyond the tithe. Finally, you will learn proven principles for eliminating debt and increasing your income. Once you have completed the book, you will have the knowledge necessary to get out of debt, improve your financial situation and have a greater impact on the growth of the Kingdom of God here on earth.

You can use this book for individual study or there are discussion questions at the end of each chapter, which allows you to use the book for a group study. If you aren't already involved in a small 'group, why not gather together a few friends who are all interested in improving their financial situation and read through the book together. You can answer the discussion questions ahead of time and then discuss them each time your group meets. This will give God another avenue to speak into your lives and you can pray for each other, which increases the power of this book.

The most exciting part is that everything in this book is solidly based in God's Word, the Bible, and proven over many years of implementation. It is all God's truth and promises to His children. If you do what God is teaching, you will prosper in all aspects of your life. So, take your time while reading this book. Underline, highlight, dog-ear pages, put sticky notes in key spots, take notes, and most of all meditate over the words that are contained in this book. God will reveal His specific financial plan for you!

CHAPTER ONE:
MINDSET AND BELIEF

I grew up in a middle-class American family living in the suburbs of Denver, Colorado. My dad worked an office job and mom stayed home with my brother and me. We never lacked, but we also never had a lot. I followed in my father's footsteps by graduating from high school, then got my college degree, and landed a good job with Motorola. I had adopted the prevalent mindset of the day and that led me to the same type of lifestyle I grew up with – just enough.

You see, like the rest of the middle and lower class, my parents were wonderful, but they had a poverty mindset. We thought that rich people were dishonest and made all their money on the backs of others. Derogatory comments were made about people driving luxury cars or living in large houses. I was envious of that lifestyle, but my mindset told me it was wrong. Growing up we always shopped for the best deal and bought the cheapest items. My mom put patches on holes in my jeans and my clothes were passed down to my younger brother. I remember wanting some white Puma football shoes (they were the rage at that time, because of Joe Namath) with a yellow formstrip, but they were too expensive, so I got a cheap pair of shoes and used a yellow acrylic paint for the formstrip. I did develop a lot of my creativity and ingenuity back then.

I carried this poverty mentality into my life and found that cheap items break quickly, and I had to buy them again and again. I was never able to save for anything and later in life, I learned to use credit cards to improve my life (or so the TV ads promised). Even after I got saved, I carried that poverty mindset into my new life. I couldn't afford to tithe and give. I walked or drove past the poor thinking that if I gave them money, it would be wasted on alcohol, drugs, or cigarettes. When the church asked for money, I figured that all the rich people would give, so I didn't have to. Does any of this sound familiar? If it does, then perhaps you too have a poverty mindset.

This poverty mindset led me to follow the world's financial advice and plan. The world's system told me that if I got that expensive college degree and the good job, I would prosper. I could climb the corporate ladder, work forty years, and retire with a nice pension that would lead to years of joyful retirement. It turned out that was a lie. Six years into my corporate career I had excelled at my job and yet I was still barely paying the bills. I was stopped on the corporate ladder by people above me with higher seniority. It occurred to me that unless I was willing to move out of state, I would be stuck in that same job for many years.

It was about that time that I was introduced to entrepreneurship through a company called Amway. Now, before you close the book, this isn't an Amway presentation or even a pitch for MLM. It's just the vehicle through which my mind was opened to something beyond the world's financial system. I was also introduced to some of God's financial plan during those years. Now, Amway has been a wonderful financial vehicle for many people, but it wasn't for me. However, it did totally open my eyes and allowed God to direct me down a new path, leading to where I am today.

In short, that moment in time changed my mindset and beliefs. For the first time in my life, I was open to the idea of prosperity and wealth, rather than just getting by. By seeing and hearing about other normal people prospering, my mind was opened to what Jesus referred to in John 10:10 as the abundant life. Now, I wish I could say that I got the revelation, and it resulted in massive wealth, but it didn't. In fact, compared to truly wealthy people in the world, I wouldn't be considered financially rich, but my wife, Karen, and I are rich in the Kingdom of God. More on that later.

Let's jump back to John 10:10 and talk about the abundant life that Jesus died for, so you could enjoy it. The NKJV reads, "*The thief does not come except to steal, and to kill, and to destroy. I have come that they may have life, and that they may have it more abundantly*." Satan/the devil/the thief has created the world's system through people he controls. It's a system of greed that is designed to steal from you, kill you, and destroy everything in your life. We see this in the wealthy people who have it all and yet they commit suicide, become drug addicts or alcoholics. Satan's system worked and he is winning in many lives.

Now, before we go too far, I want to stress that we still live in this world and God can still use the worldly vehicles such as jobs, businesses, the stock market, commodities, crypto currencies, and the internet to prosper His kids. There is a difference between operating fully within the world's system and just using worldly vehicles under the direction of God. That's what you will learn in this book.

The second part of John 10:10 is where we want to focus. It's the abundant life that Jesus presents to all believers through his death. Let's begin by examining the definition of abundant. Merriam-Webster Dictionary defines abundant as: "existing or occurring in large amounts, marked by great plenty, and amply supplied or abounding." Do you see any lack in there? The abundant life has no lack and it's what God intends for your life if you operate fully in His financial plan.

The first step to enter God's financial plan is to

transform that poverty mindset into an abundance mindset. Romans 12:2 teaches this principle of transforming your mind, "*Do not conform to the pattern of this world, but be transformed by the renewing of your mind. Then you will be able to test and approve what God's will is—his good, pleasing and perfect will.*" You and I are transformed by the renewing of our minds. We must allow God to change the way we think.

Let's start with why we spend money. Most people spend a lot of money trying to look good and impress other people, yet it's more important how God sees you. The answer is to stop spending money to impress ourselves or others and start being generous toward God. He loves a generous giver!

Next, let's examine the word prosperity. In 2001, when God gave these financial principles to my spiritual mentor, Tim Johnson and I, prosperity was literally a bad word in the church. Whenever we spoke and mentioned prosperity, people would complain. We didn't understand why because God uses the word in His Bible many times. In fact, it's used 111 times in the NLT, 101 times in the NKJV, 91 times in the KJV, and 84 times in the NIV. I happen to think that if God mentions something once in the Bible, it's important. God mentions prosperity many times in the translations of His Word. It must be very important and something He wants us to learn about.

In the introduction I mentioned Jeremiah 29:11, "'*For I know the plans I have for you,' declares the* LORD, *'plans to prosper you and not to harm you, plans to give you hope and a future.'*" God has a plan to prosper you. How can that be bad or wrong? Clearly God doesn't have an issue with prosperity, so neither should we.

The problem is that the world also uses the word prosperity in exchange for material wealth – the accumulation of money and things – greed. Once again, that's satan at work distorting something that God meant for the good of mankind. Again, as mentioned in the introduction, prosperity means not lacking anything. If you can't pay the bills, you are either living above your means, which I will address later in the book, or you aren't operating in God's financial plan. God's plan is to prosper you in every area of life. Jesus came to give you abundant life, which includes your finances. Don't let anything or anyone tell you otherwise.

Still not convinced? Let's study another scripture, 3 John 1:2 (NKJV), "*Beloved, I pray that you may prosper in all things and be in health, just as your soul prospers.*" Would your finances be included in "all things"? The correct answer is "YES"! The Greek word translated as prosper is Euodoo, which means to cause to prosper or be successful. The Apostle John, under the inspiration of the Holy Spirit, is saying that God wants you to prosper or be successful in all things. God wants you to be successful financially.

Let's go back to the last part of John 10:10 and study the Greek word that is translated as abundantly and see how it fits into this picture of prosperity. That word is *perissos*, which means exceeding your need or more than enough. In other words, God doesn't want to give you just enough so you can scrape by. He wants to go far beyond your basic needs, so you can be a blessing to others and help build His Kingdom on earth. God wants your finances to overflow.

That reminds me of a story about a beloved king who threw a party and asked everyone in his kingdom to attend. The admittance fee was water for the moat. On the day of the party, people arrived with cups of water, buckets, and even animal troughs full. No matter how much water they brought, they were admitted to the party. It was a luxurious event complete with a magnificent feast, music, entertainment, and dancing. As the evening concluded, the king arose and spoke. He thanked all of them for attending the party and said he had one final gift. The king waved his hand to the back of the room and two men opened two very large wood doors. Inside was the king's treasury filled with gold, silver, and jewels. He told the people that they could take as much treasure as would fit in the container in which they brought water. Those with cups were quite disappointed, whereas those with animal troughs were very pleased. Each person packed their container with treasure, pressing and shaking it down, until it was overflowing.

Luke 6:38 tells a similar story, *"Give, and it will be given to you. A good measure, pressed down, shaken together and running over, will be poured into your lap. For with the measure you use, it will be measured to you."* What measure are you using to give to the King of kings? Are you using a cup, a bucket, or an animal trough? The interesting part is that God always gives back greater value than what you give. In the story, each person gave water, but left with valuable treasure. God will give back to you according to how you give, but will always give you more than what you gave.

Let's study this further in 2 Corinthians 9, where it's very clear that the Apostle Paul is talking about a financial offering and generosity. In verse 6, Paul says, *"Remember this: Whoever sows sparingly will also reap sparingly, and whoever sows generously will also reap generously."* He's speaking of sowing financial seeds that will grow into a financial harvest. I will dig deeper into this in Chapter Four.

In verse 7, Paul describes the proper giving attitude, *"Each of you should give what you have decided in your heart to give, not reluctantly or under compulsion, for God loves a cheerful giver."* There are three mindset keys in this scripture. First is that we are to give what we have decided in our heart. Paul isn't talking about your blood pumping heart, but rather your spirit. It means that if you are spiritually aligned with God, then your thoughts will move toward generosity. It's often said that people have a generous heart. That's because they are aligned with God's heart, which is always generous.

When you have opportunities to give, seek God for an amount. Karen and I often attend conferences that have multiple opportunities to give. We pray leading up to the conferences and pray at offering time. There are times when we both get the same amount and other times when Karen has a higher amount. I've found that if we get two amounts, the lowest one is my greedy flesh (I'm still a work in process) and the higher one is always God. Give the higher amount and God will bless that offering.

The second mindset key in verse 7 of 2 Corinthians 9 is that we are not to give reluctantly or under compulsion. If we listen to all the Christian teachers who are anti-prosperity, we will develop that poverty mindset I mentioned earlier. Out of that mindset, we will question motives for the offering, such as, what they are going to do with the money? If we give under those circumstances, it will be reluctantly or under compulsion. God can't bless that offering, so we might as well keep the money. We are made in God's image and so we give because God is the ultimate giver. He loved us so much that He gave His only begotten Son to redeem us. We give because He gives.

The third mindset in verse 7 is that we are to give cheerfully. Right now, when you write that tithe check or give an offering, how do you feel? Are you filled with joy or fear? The Greek word that is translated as cheerful is *hilaros*, which is where we get our word hilarious. Out of our love for God and a mindset of generosity, we should give hilariously. What if during offering time everyone was cheering like they do at a football game? That would be hilarious giving.

We recently experienced a time of hilarious giving at our church, AZ Vineyard. We had been renting a building for many years and had an opportunity to buy it. The financial institution wanted us to have $37,000 in a savings account, as an emergency fund. We only had $27,000, so we appealed to our small congregation for the extra $10,000. Wow were we surprised by the generous response, as we saw $37,000 come in and we didn't even have to touch our savings. These are people who have an abundance mindset.

Let's move on to 2 Corinthians 9:8 where God gives us some promises, "*And God is able to bless you abundantly, so that in all things at all times, having all that you need, you will abound in every good work.*" When you give generously and cheerfully, then God can bless you abundantly. You will then have plenty of money for two things – your needs and to give more.

Let's finish this thought in verses 10 through 12 of 2 Corinthians 9. Verse 10 reads, "Now he who supplies seed to the sower and bread for food will also supply and increase your store of seed and will enlarge the harvest of your righteousness." God supplies all our financial seed. Some of that seed is for food, which means to take care of our needs and wants. Now, if you are living above your means, then you are using too much of your seed for needs and wants and won't have any seed to plant for a future harvest. According to verse 10, if you correctly use the financial seed God gives you, He will give you more. That's the abundant life.

Verse 11 is a very challenging scripture for the "it's holy to be poor" teachers. It reads, "*You will be enriched in every way so that you can be generous on every occasion, and through us your generosity will result in thanksgiving to God.*" The Greek word that is translated as enriched is *ploutizo*, which means to make rich. What? The Apostle Paul is telling the Corinthian church that they will be made rich in EVERY way, so they can be generous on EVERY occasion and that through their generosity, other people will give thanks to God. For example, if you generously give to a ministry that feeds hungry children in Africa, those kids and their parents, will give thanks to God for your gift. Wow! If you go and feed the homeless in your area, they will give thanks to God for the food. As a Pastor, I often give thanks for the generosity of our congregation, which enables us to do the work of the Lord.

In full transparency, I have had plenty of opportunities to give, but didn't have the money to do so. I remember one time when Karen and I were in Nanaimo, Canada speaking at a business event on Saturday night. We stayed that night in the hotel and on Sunday morning wanted to go to church. As we exited the elevator, we heard what sounded like worship music and traced it to one of the meeting rooms, where we found a group of people preparing for a church service. After a nice breakfast at the hotel, we joined them for the service. After some worship, the pastor spoke about the opportunity they had to buy a building. He said they needed $30,000 and my first thought was that I wished I could write a $30,000 check and put it in the offering basket. I even imagined them counting the offering - $20, $100, $50, $30,000… What?

I want to be that kind of generous and hilarious giver. How about you? God is looking for people He can bless, who will use what He gives them to bless others. He wants to enrich (make rich) you so that you can be generous in every situation. Then you can bless your relatives or friends who are experiencing financial struggle. You can help that single mom with three kids to make ends meet. You can feed some homeless people. You can fund ministries and missionaries and help expand the Kingdom of God. Your giving will result in thanksgiving to God and Him being magnified on the earth.

Let's move on to some common financial myths that have hindered Christians and the Church. These must be dispelled and removed from our thinking if we are going to operate in God's financial plan.

Myth #1: It's Holy to Be Poor

The first myth is that it's holy to be poor. People who perpetuate this myth always seem to quote 2 Corinthians 8:9 (NLT), "*You know the generous grace of our Lord Jesus Christ. Though he was rich, yet for your sakes he became poor...*" They use this scripture to say that Jesus was poor, and we should be also. That's the devil talking. The problem is that those who advocate the holy-to-be-poor lifestyle apparently didn't read the rest of 2 Corinthians 8:9, "*so that by his poverty he could make you rich.*" If we took this at face value, Jesus wants us rich, but if we look at the scripture in context, it's not speaking of money, rather it's addressing spiritual riches.

Jesus became spiritually poor by giving up the glories of heaven and his godly attributes to be born as a flesh and blood human baby. He did that so that we could become rich, referencing salvation and eternal life. Setting that aside, Jesus, as an adult, wasn't poor spiritually or physically. He had the Holy Spirit in him, which made him rich. He also wasn't financially poor, as he was wearing a seamless robe that only the wealthy wore. He also had many wealthy people following him, who were supporting his ministry. He had a treasurer who was stealing and yet no one except Jesus seemed to know. Finally, he had a lot of followers that he had to support. Jesus was rich spiritually and financially and that's what he intends for his true disciples today.

Myth #2: Money is the Root of All Evil

I've encountered many believers and non-believers who think they are quoting the Bible when they say that money is the root of all evil. This, of course, is a misquotation of 1 Timothy 6:10, "*For the love of money is a root of all kinds of evil. Some people, eager for money, have wandered from the faith and pierced themselves with many griefs.*" Money is just a resource. It's not good or bad. God doesn't want us loving money and material things. He wants us to love Him and use money to build the Kingdom on earth. If we prove that we can do that, He will give us increasing amounts of money.

Myth #3: It's Either Money or God, but Not Both

This is a misinterpretation of Matthew 6:24 (NLT), "*No one can serve two masters. For you will hate one and love the other; you will be devoted to one and despise the other. You cannot serve both God and money.*" This doesn't say you can't have both, it says you can't serve both. The question is, "who is your master – money and materialism or God?" If your mind is constantly focused on money and what it can buy, that's your master. If you are focused on God, He will provide ways for you to earn money and as you use the money to further the Kingdom and help those in need, He will give you more. You actually can have both God and money.

These are just three of the most common myths. There are others and if you encounter them, always apply the Word of God to dispel the myth. God wants our minds to be focused on Him and what He's doing. He recognizes that life and ministry require money, so He needs His kids to be prosperous. Now, God isn't going to grow a money tree in your back yard or rain down money inside your house; I know, because I've asked many times. Rather, God wants us to be like Jesus, with an abundance mindset. Let's look at some examples:

When faced with a wedding feast disaster – no more wine – Jesus turned water into fine wine (John 2:1-11). When needing to feed 5,000 and 4,000 hungry men, plus women and children, Jesus blessed a few small loaves and fishes. Everyone was fed until full and there was plenty left over (Matthew 14:13-21 and Matthew 15:29-39). When asked to pay the temple tax, Jesus sent Peter to fish and pull a coin from the fish's mouth (Matthew 17:27). When the disciples were panicking over what they would eat and wear, Jesus told them not to worry and to look at the birds and the flowers. All they had to do was seek first the Kingdom of God and His righteousness and everything they needed would be provided (Matthew 6:25-34). Apparently, that must have worked for the disciples, as they never seemed to be in lack. It will also work for Jesus' true disciples today.

1 Corinthians 2:16 tells us that we have the mind of Christ. This is not our natural mind, but rather our spiritual mind. The mind of Christ has an abundance mindset, so all we have to do is tap into

it, instead of our natural mind. According to Romans 12:2, this requires transforming the mind with the Word of God. As we fill our natural mind with God's Word, it will transform into a mind that is in sync with the spiritual mind. We will then begin thinking more like Jesus, which results in acting more like him as well.

Before we wrap up this chapter, I have a caution about mindset. God wants us to have an abundance mentality, so that He can flow finances through us. There's the key, through us. He's not looking for reservoirs; people who hoard the money and use it for their own pleasures. Rather, He's looking for rivers; people who let the money flow through them into Kingdom work. Now, don't go overboard on this, God doesn't mind if you have a nice home, drive a nice car, have nice things, travel, etc. He just doesn't want those to become idols that pull you away from Him.

In Luke 12:13-21, Jesus cautioned the crowd about this. In verse 15, he tells them, "*Watch out! Be on guard against all kinds of greed; life does not consist in an abundance of possessions.*" Jesus then goes on to tell the parable of the rich man. This man is storing up wealth for himself and his pleasures. Unfortunately, he died and couldn't enjoy any of it. Jesus ends the parable by saying, "This is how it will be with whoever stores up things for themselves, but is not rich toward God." God expects His disciples to be rich toward the Kingdom and helping the poor.

If I were to examine your home, vehicles, bank account, garage, basement, attic or storage unit, would it look like you were storing things for yourself or being rich toward God? I spent many years storing things for my own purposes, only to see them drift away. Through the years, God has been working on renewing my mind in the area of being rich toward God. He doesn't need our money, but He does want our entire heart. Matthew 6:21 (NLT) reads, "*Wherever your treasure is, there the desires of your heart will also be.*" Where is your heart? Is it focused on gaining wealth or more intimacy with God?

Also, do you have a mindset for expansion and increase? When I first learned to give, my spiritual mentor encouraged me to tithe (10%) and give 10% above the tithe. Once I got there, he encouraged me to increase it to 15%, then 20%, and so on. There are Christians out there who have learned to live on 10 - 20% of their income and give the rest.

The great news about mindset is that God can change it. I recently read a story about a couple who were challenged to give $1 million a year. Because they gave $17,000 the previous year, which was 35% of their income, they thought a million dollars was impossible. The person challenging them said, well than how about $50,000 this year. They thought the person was joking, because they only made $50,000 last year, but he encouraged them to believe God for it.

They opened their minds to the possibility and God gave them ideas and favor and sure enough, they were able to give $50,000. The next year they gave $100,000 and within a few years they were up to $1 million. God expanded their mindset, and He can do the same for you. If we open our minds to God's way of doing things, He will do more than we could ever imagine or expect.

As we conclude this chapter, just a quick reminder that God doesn't expect us to be poor, as that doesn't work for spreading the Kingdom. He also doesn't want us to make money an idol and begin to love money more than Him. As we expand our mindset on money and prove to God that we can utilize what He gives us, He will give us more. His greatest expectation is that we use the money He gives us to tithe, take care of our basic needs, save a little for emergencies, and then use the rest to help those in need and further Kingdom work on earth. Over the last twenty-five years, I've gained a much better mindset and belief in God as my abundant provider. I certainly haven't arrived and still struggle at times, but God is doing a good work and He will do the same in your mindset and belief.

CHAPTER ONE: ACTIVATION

Personal Activities

1. List 5 things your parents (or you now) used to or currently say about rich people.
2. Find 10 scriptures that speak about prosperity, abundance, riches, and wealth in a positive way and begin memorizing those.

Small Group Discussion Questions

1. What are some ways you can tell you have a poverty mindset?
2. Why does God want His children to prosper financially?
3. Discuss the 3 myths and whether you have struggled with any of them.
4. Discuss some ways that you could be more generous with the money God provides.

CHAPTER TWO:
STEWARDSHIP

Stewardship is an interesting topic, as in our current culture we don't talk or teach about it and there are few examples. Dictionary.com defines steward as "a person who manages another's property or financial affairs; one who administers anything as an agent of another or others." For the purpose of this book, we are going to define a steward as a person who handles God's wealth as if it were their own.

Stewardship was established at the beginning of mankind. Genesis 2:15 reads, *"The LORD God took the man and put him in the Garden of Eden to work it and take care of it."* We so often read that Adam was to "work it", as labor, but in the beginning, God had created a system that was self-producing. All the trees and plants were seed bearing, so they produced their own new crop. Working by the sweat of the brow came later through the curse.

According to Genesis 2:15, Adam's job was to

"work it". That is the root meaning of the Hebrew word *abad* (aw-bad) which is translated as "work it". He was to serve God by watching over or guarding God's earth and the animals on it, which is the meaning of the Hebrew word *shamar* (shaw-mar') that translates as "take care of it". So, Adam's job was to serve God by stewarding the earth.

The key to understanding stewardship is to recognize that God owns everything. Psalm 24:1 (NASB) reads: "*The earth is the LORD's, and all it contains, the world, and those who dwell in it.*" God owns the land, water, trees, plants, animals, and people.

Quite often I'll be in a conversation, and mention something about my house or car. I'll bet you've done the same thing. Yet, by what we just learned, that house or car belongs to the Lord. We don't own anything. God owns it all and let's us use His stuff.

This book is about finances, but I'm going to digress a bit to help us understand God's plan for stewardship. The Bible clearly teaches that we are to be stewards of four things (and only one of them is money):

God's Grace

The last part of 1 Peter 4:10 says: "*...as faithful stewards of God's grace in its various forms.*" The Son of God gave up the glories of heaven, set aside His Godly attributes and allowed Himself to be confined to the flesh and blood body of a helpless baby. He had to grow in wisdom and stature, as we do. He was tempted in every way, as we are. Finally, he, the Son of Man, submitted himself to horrendous torture, humiliation, and crucifixion to bring God's grace to the earth. He is the only path to heaven and eternity with God. We are to be stewards of that grace. In other words, God expects us to share that gift of grace with everyone we meet.

I must admit that I struggle a bit in this area of stewardship. That probably sounds strange coming from a pastor, but I have the same fears as any other person. Fear that I won't say the right thing or in the right way. Fear that they will ask something I can't answer. Fear that they will get mad and even yell at me. Fear that it will damage the relationship. These fears have kept me from properly stewarding God's grace. Perhaps you have had these same struggles.

Oh, I've shared the gospel with many people through sermons, messages, via social media, and in my books, but I'm not great face-to-face. God is working on my faith in that area. I want to be a good steward of God's grace. How about you?

God's Gifts

The first part of 1 Peter 4:10 covers this one: "*Each of you should use whatever gift you have received to serve others…*" This is talking about spiritual gifts which can be found in Romans 12:6-8; 1 Corinthians 12:8-10 & 28; and Ephesians 4:11. These gifts came with the Holy Spirit when he took up residence in your spirit at the time of salvation.

God uses them through you to accomplish His purposes on earth.

The Apostle Paul says that we should eagerly desire the greater gifts in 1 Corinthians 12:31. We can't be good stewards of God's gifts if we are ignorant of them. So, the first step is to discover your gifts. There are many good spiritual gifts assessments on the internet. Just do a search for spiritual gifts assessment or test and you will find them. I would suggest taking several of them and comparing the results. Look for the common results.

We have all the gifts, but usually two or three that are stronger. That can change as your ministry needs change. Once you have a good idea of your primary gifts, then speak with your pastor or another Christian leader about how to best steward those gifts to serve the body of Christ.

Time

God doesn't operate in time. He experiences what we call past, present, and future at the same time. A rudimentary illustration of this is the difference between seeing a very long train from the air, where you see it all, and watching one car rumble by at a time. God see's your whole life and you see it one moment at a time.

The Bible doesn't specifically say we are to steward time, but the concept can be found in Proverbs 6:6-11, Ecclesiastes 3:1-13, and Ephesians 5:15-21.

These all talk about how we use our time and it's important to use it as God intended.

Time is the great equalizer. We all get the same amount of time each day. The homeless and the billionaire all get 1,440 minutes each day. It's what they do with their time that makes the difference. How are you stewarding the time that God gives you?

The best way to steward your time is to give God the first fruits of your day. When you get up each morning, give God the first of your time – read the Bible, worship, and pray. Think of it this way. God has already seen your day. He knows everything that will happen. Why wouldn't you want to meet with him in the morning and allow Him to prepare you for the day. Now, He's not going to tell you exactly what will happen, but He will prepare your heart and give you scriptures for everything you will encounter in that day. Also, you can ask Him for wisdom and protection for the day. Then, throughout the day, stay in conversation with Him, so He can lead and guide.

Money

Is money important to God? Howard Dayton, co-founder of Crown Financial Ministries, compiled a topical overview of 2,350 verses that comment on the handling of money and material possessions. I've always figured that if God put a topic in the Bible once, it was important. Since God felt it necessary to address money and possessions 2,350 times, it must be important, and we should invest the time to gain His perspective on money.

Since all the money belongs to God and He gives us some of His money to use, He expects us to be good stewards of it. Let's look at an example of that in Matthew 25:14-30 (NKJV), also known as the parable of the talents:

> *"For the kingdom of heaven is like a man traveling to a far country, who called his own servants and delivered his goods to them. And to one he gave five talents, to another two, and to another one, to each according to his own ability; and immediately he went on a journey. Then he who had received the five talents went and traded with them, and made another five talents. And likewise he who had received two gained two more also. But he who had received one went and dug in the ground, and hid his lord's money. After a long time the lord of those servants came and settled accounts with them.*

> *"So, he who had received five talents came and brought five other talents, saying, 'Lord, you delivered to me five talents; look, I have gained five more talents besides them.' His lord*

said to him, 'Well done, good and faithful servant; you were faithful over a few things, I will make you ruler over many things. Enter into the joy of your lord.' He also who had received two talents came and said, 'Lord, you delivered to me two talents; look, I have gained two more talents besides them.' His lord said to him, 'Well done, good and faithful servant; you have been faithful over a few things, I will make you ruler over many things. Enter into the joy of your lord.'

"Then he who had received the one talent came and said, 'Lord, I knew you to be a hard man, reaping where you have not sown, and gathering where you have not scattered seed. And I was afraid, and went and hid your talent in the ground. Look, there you have what is yours.'

"But his lord answered and said to him, 'You wicked and lazy servant, you knew that I reap where I have not sown, and gather where I have not scattered seed. So you ought to have deposited my money with the bankers, and at my coming I would have received back my own with interest. Therefore take the talent *from him, and give it to him who has ten talents.*

'For to everyone who has, more will be given, and he will have abundance; but from him who does not have, even what he has will be taken away. And cast the unprofitable servant into the outer darkness. There will be weeping and gnashing of teeth.'"

This is one of my favorite parables in the Bible. We all want to hear the "Well done, good and faithful servant", right? So, let's dig into the scripture and determine what must be done to hear that from our Lord.

First, because we use the word talent in a different way than they did when Jesus told this parable, let's define what the Bible calls talent. It was a Greek unit of weight – approximately 80 pounds. It was also a unit of currency and was worth about 6,000 denarii. A denarii was the usual pay for a day's labor, so, if we do the math, a talent is equivalent to sixteen and a half years of labor. Needless to say, the servants in this parable were entrusted with a lot of money.

Jesus tells the parable of the talents to show us that He expects us to be good stewards of the money God gives us. Jesus is the man traveling to a faraway country (heaven) and we are the servants he has entrusted with money.

Notice in verse 15 that the man entrusts different amounts of money according to the servant's ability to handle it. God looks at how we handle money and then allows us to have only what we can properly handle. For example, no parent in their right mind would give a one-year-old a $100 bill. A child has no concept of value, and it would probably go right into their mouth. Now, a teenager understands the value of the $100 bill, but most haven't been trained to properly steward money, so they will likely blow it on selfish purchases. On the other hand, a mature adult Christian, who has received proper biblical teaching about handling money, will likely give a good portion of that $100 to help the needy and further the Kingdom, because they understand the principle of stewardship.

It's interesting that the man, who is going away, tells the two servants who achieved increase, the same thing – "*Well done, good and faithful servant; you were faithful over a few things, I will make you ruler over many things. Enter into the joy of the Lord.*" This means that God is rewarding good stewardship (increase), not performance.

In contrast, the man is angry with his servant who buried or didn't invest the money he was given. In our case, it would be the misuse of God's money. This happens when Christians don't tithe and give offerings. Now, here's the scary part. According to recent research studies, Christians are only giving about 2.5% of what they make and that's down from 3.3% during the Great Depression! Clearly, we are not being good stewards of God's money.

If those who are committed Christians would just tithe (10% of their gross income), it would add approximately $165 billion into Kingdom work. We could relieve global hunger, eliminate homelessness, solve the world's water and sanitation issues and fully fund the Great Commission, with a lot left over to do other ministry work.

Okay, back to the parable of the talents. The good news is in the first part of verse 29, *"For to everyone who has, more will be given, and he will have abundance..."* In other words, if we are good stewards of God's money, He will give us more and we will enjoy abundance. There is an old saying that you can't out give God and that is so true. When we handle His money well, He loves to bless us with even more.

So, what does good stewardship of money look like. In the balance of this chapter, I'm going to give you a cursory introduction to the concept, and we will dig deeper in the coming chapters.

Tithe

The word tithe means 10%. Since 100% of the money you receive, belongs to God, a proper tithe is 10% of all money you receive. That would include your salary, bonuses, commissions, and gifts. Your gross income is the amount you receive before any deductions (withholding, insurance, 401k, etc). Tithing is the first and most critical step in proper stewardship of money.

Tithing is really a lordship issue. Will we make Jesus Lord over our money? If so, we will cheerfully tithe and trust God to do more with the 90% than we could with the 100%. I'm going to teach heavily on and share some great stories about tithing in Chapter Five. In that chapter I will deal with all the typical questions and concerns about tithing as a New Testament Christian. Right now, I just want you to know that tithing is part of stewardship and to understand some of the benefits.

I'll cover Malachi 3:8-11 more extensively in Chapter Five, but, let's take a quick look at what God is saying in verses 10 and 11:

> "*'Bring the whole tithe into the <u>storehouse</u>, that there may be <u>food</u> in my house. <u>Test me in this</u>,' says the* LORD *Almighty, 'and see if I will not <u>throw open the floodgates of heaven</u> and pour out so much blessing that there will not be room enough to store it. ¹¹ I will <u>prevent pests from devouring your crops</u>, and the vines in your fields will not drop their fruit before it is ripe," says the* LORD *Almighty.'"* (emphasis added)

As we analyze the scripture, I've underlined some key parts. First, the tithe goes to the storehouse. When this scripture was written, people brought animals, grain, and fruit as their tithe. The temple had a storehouse where the tithe was kept. Today we bring money, and the tithe is brought to the church building. The tithe is to cover the operational expenses of the church (building, salaries, equipment, furniture, etc), so that the food of the Word can be given to those who want it. If Christians stop tithing, one day we may find ourselves with no church buildings and no place for people to go and receive the Word-food and sometimes even actual food.

Next, God says something that is really amazing. It's the only place in the Bible where I've found that He says this. "*Test Me in this*." Wow, God is actually telling us to test Him to see what He will do. Then, He tells us what He will do if we tithe.

The first promise is that, if we tithe, God will "*throw open the floodgates of heaven and pour out so much blessing that there will not be room enough to store it*." Next, God says that He will protect the rest of what He's given you (90%) from the devourer (satan and his demonic hoard). This means that our 90% will go further than the 100% would have, if we didn't tithe.

I have taught biblical finances for over 20 years and have heard many people, who began to tithe, say that they couldn't figure out how it worked. Their income didn't increase, and bills didn't decrease, yet, there was suddenly money left over. That's because God protected the 90% and it went further than the 100% did, before they tithed. Now, keep in mind that this isn't some kind of magic formula that works every time. There will still be financial struggles at times (particularly if we misuse God's money or we have a bad attitude about tithing and giving). The good news is that no matter what happens, God will lead you through.

Now, you may be thinking that you can't afford to tithe. I can relate. For many years after Karen and I got saved, we didn't tithe. We were deeply in debt (more on that later) and were having trouble just making our payments. Can you relate? However, once we gained solid understanding of the importance of tithing, we took that leap of faith and have been tithing ever since. The cool part is that although we have had some very difficult financial times, since we began tithing, we have always had all of our needs met.

The final thought I want to leave you with in this segment, is that if you don't want to be ruled by money (love of money, making money your god), tithe and give. Generosity is the perfect antidote to greed and generosity begins with the tithe.

If you aren't currently tithing, then you aren't being a good steward of God's money. I highly recommend that when you get paid, you write the first check to God (or immediately give 10%

through online or text giving). Test God and see what He does!

Offering

Tithing is the first step in good stewardship of money. Next is the offering, which is what we give above and beyond the tithe. Malachi 3:8 makes it very clear that both the tithe and offering are important to God:

> *"'Will a mere mortal rob God? Yet you rob me. But you ask, 'How are we robbing you?' 'In tithes and offerings.'"* (emphasis added)

I don't know how you feel, but I don't want to rob God, so I both tithe and give offerings. As we discussed in the previous section, the tithe always goes to the church where you are being fed the Word of God (sermons, classes, Bible studies, etc.). Offerings can be given to your church, other churches, ministries, or to people in need.

The tithe amount is fixed at 10%, but the offering is arbitrary. According to 2 Corinthians 9:7, we are to give what God puts on our heart. When offering time comes, ask God how much above the tithe you should give. If you are getting two numbers, most likely the higher one is God. Once you have an amount, give cheerfully, not under compulsion or obligation. When you give this way, God can bless you with more.

This same principle is true when you encounter ministries that feed, clothe, dig water wells, take Bibles into other countries, free people caught in sex trafficking and those who have been ensnared by the sex industry. Also, when you encounter someone in need – homeless, single moms, widows, and orphans. Ask God how you can best help them.

After Karen and I began to tithe, my spiritual mentor challenged me to begin giving offerings that totaled an additional 10% of my gross income. This was at the time when we felt we couldn't afford to tithe and God taught us, that with His math, He could make it work and He did. However, we didn't have an additional 10% to give as an offering. Again, God had to do some work on our faith, but we finally decided to trust Him and began giving offerings that totaled 10% above our tithe.

We now give to three major ministries every month, sponsor two children through World Vision and Compassion International, give to individuals in and outside our church, and help out when needs arise. God always provides more than enough, so we have money left over.

So, from this week forward, if you aren't tithing, begin tithing. If you are already tithing, start giving offerings above your tithe and build that up to 10%. Once you reach 10%, set a new, higher goal of giving. God will always honor that!

I love this quote from Winston Churchill, "We

make a living by what we get; we make a life by what we give." Become a cheerful and generous giver.

God expects us to be good stewards of His grace, gifts, time, and money. If you are a born-again believer, you have the Holy Spirit living in you. He will guide you through the process of learning to be a good steward. Listen for that still small voice. Study the Word of God, as it is filled with great advice and many fun stories about stewardship.

God's financial plan is activated by stewardship. As you steward God's grace, He will connect you with key people who need to know Him. Some of those may contribute to His financial plan for you. Becoming a good steward of your spiritual gifts will enable you to tap into God's plans, see where He is working, and hear what He is saying. His plans are always greater than our plans. As you steward the time God gives you, you will accomplish more in the same amount of time. Finally, as you steward money effectively, God will reward you with more. Don't put it off, start today!

CHAPTER TWO: ACTIVATION

Personal Activities

1. Evaluate how much you gave in the previous year and then set a challenging giving goal for this year; something that only God could do and then begin to give that way.

2. In the lesson read the four things that we are to be stewards of and then rate yourself 1 (low) to 10 (high) in each of those areas. Now make a plan to increase your score in each.

Small Group Discussion Questions

1. How did the chapter define stewardship?
2. According to this chapter, what are some areas that we are to be stewards of? How are you doing in each of those areas?
3. Based on the parable of the talents and your current giving, would you say you are a 5 talent, 2 talent, or a 1 talent person? How can you improve?
4. If our Master (Jesus) were to return and you gave an account of how you handled His money, how do you think He would respond?
5. Are you a tither? Giver above the tithe? If not, why?

CHAPTER THREE:
PARTNERSHIP

God works in partnership – Father, Son, and Holy Spirit. He also loves to work in partnership with mankind. We see this from Genesis (Adam and Eve) through Revelation (John). God's financial plan is not a solo act. If you are trying to be the lone ranger, you're going to fail. You need both God and other people to become financially successful.

Ecclesiastes 4:9-12 shows us God's view of partnership:

> *"Two are better than one, because they have a good return for their labor: If either of them falls down, one can help the other up. But pity anyone who falls and has no one to help them up. Also, if two lie down together, they will keep warm. But how can one keep warm alone? Though one may be overpowered,*

> *two can defend themselves. A cord of*
> *three strands is not quickly broken."*

We see in Ecclesiastes that there are great benefits in partnership, and I will discuss each of those a little later. Just know that God's plan is for partnership here on earth. It's how He will fulfill His purpose for each of us and our world.

Let's look at the original partnership, starting in Genesis 1:1-3:

> *"In the beginning God created the*
> *heavens and the earth. Now the earth*
> *was formless and empty, darkness*
> *was over the surface of the deep, and*
> *the Spirit of God was hovering over*
> *the waters. And God said, "Let there*
> *be light," and there was light."*

In this scripture, we see God (Father), Spirit of God (Holy Spirit), and God speaking (Son). How do we know this last one is the Son? Let's read John 1:1-3 and 14:

> *"In the beginning was the Word, and*
> *the Word was with God, and the*
> *Word was God. He was with God in*
> *the beginning. Through him all*
> *things were made; without him*
> *nothing was made that has been*
> *made."*

> *"The Word became flesh and made his dwelling among us."*

Who is the only one who was with God and was God and then came from heaven, took on flesh and blood and dwelled among mankind? The Son of God/Jesus. So, in Genesis 1, we see the partnership of God the Father, God the Holy Spirit, and God the Son working together to create the universe, our solar system, earth, and all living creatures, including mankind.

Now let's look at God's partnership with mankind in Genesis 1:26-28:

> *Then God said, "Let us make mankind in our image, in our likeness, so that they may rule over the fish in the sea and the birds in the sky, over the livestock and all the wild animals, and over all the creatures that move along the ground." So God created mankind in his own image, in the image of God he created them; male and female he created them. God blessed them and said to them, "Be fruitful and increase in number; fill the earth and subdue it.*

God created us in His image and likeness. He created us for partnership. In the last chapter we learned about stewardship. God created mankind to be stewards of the earth. As its Creator, God still owned the earth and everything on and in it, but He created mankind to rule and subdue.

The Hebrew word that is translated as subdue is *kabash* (kaw-bash'), which is a military word that means to make subservient or bring into bondage. In partnership with God, mankind was given dominion over the earth and expected to conquer it. It's the same for us today. Our sinful world needs to be subdued and we can only do that through partnership with God and with each other.

We see the continuation of God's partnership all through the Old Testament – prophets, judges, kings, and a bunch of ordinary people. Into the New Testament, we see God partner with John the Baptist to announce the coming of His Son. Back to John 1 and let's look at verses 4-7:

> *"In him was life, and that life was the light of all mankind. The light shines in the darkness, and the darkness has not overcome it. There was a man sent from God whose name was John. He came as a witness to testify concerning that light, so that through him all might believe. He himself was not the light; he came only as a witness to the light."*

The Word, who is the Son of God, took on flesh and became the son of man, Jesus. He is the light of mankind. God then partnered with John the Baptist to testify that Jesus was the Word, the Son of God, the long-awaited Messiah. John made it clear that he was not the Messiah, he was just the one sent to point out the One.

Jesus then partnered with his fellow man to bring salvation to mankind in John 1:12-13:

> *"Yet to all who did receive him, to those who believed in his name, he gave the right to become children of God—children born not of natural descent, nor of human decision or a husband's will, but born of God."*

Finally, the Holy Spirit partners with man for greater power. We see the first instance of this in Matthew 3:16-17:

> *As soon as Jesus was baptized, he went up out of the water. At that moment heaven was opened, and he saw the Spirit of God descending like a dove and alighting on him. And a voice from heaven said, "This is my Son, whom I love; with him I am well pleased."*

Then we see the Holy Spirt descend upon and fill the disciples on the day of Pentecost in Acts 2:1-4:

> *"When the day of Pentecost came, they were all together in one place. Suddenly a sound like the blowing of a violent wind came from heaven and*

filled the whole house where they were sitting. They saw what seemed to be tongues of fire that separated and came to rest on each of them. All of them were filled with the Holy Spirit and began to speak in other tongues as the Spirit enabled them."

It's easy to see that God has partnered with Himself and with mankind. The Greek word translated as partner is *koinonos*, which means associate, comrade, companion, one who shares in anything. Would the disciples have been Jesus' partners? Most definitely. How about you and me? Yes, Jesus expects every born-again believer to be his partner in furthering the Kingdom on earth.

Let's examine the four stages of partnership with God, as outlined in John Maxwell's book, *The Power of Partnership in the Church*:

1. **Friendship** – as with any friendship, it starts when you meet a person and start getting to know them. In this stage you meet Jesus, begin reading and studying the Bible, start having prayer times, and begin trusting God.

2. **Formation** – now you begin to understand your identity in Christ. You are a child of God, co-heir with Jesus, spiritual being operating in an earth suit, citizen of heaven. During this phase, you uncover your

primary spiritual gifts and calling. You also begin to contribute to Kingdom expansion, by sharing your testimony and talking with people about Jesus.

3. **Functioning** – you partner with your local church body by serving in a ministry or possibly launching a new ministry. You may also begin to serve outside the church walls in a ministry to the poor or homeless, go on a mission trip or possibly even begin the steps to become a full-time missionary or plant a church or ministry.

4. **Fruitfulness** – in this phase you are fully operating in your giftings and calling and the fruit of your labor – new salvations and discipleship – are evident.

Next, let's examine the benefits of partnership with God:

1. **Accomplish and Earn More** – I think most of us know that we can accomplish more as part of a team than we can alone. In Ecclesiastes 4:9, King Solmon confirms this:

> *"Two are better than one, because they have a good return for their labor."*

For about ten years I owned an advertising agency. It was a great example of partnership resulting in accomplishing more. I would go out and secure the accounts. Then I would work with our creative team to come up with a plan for the account. Next, the graphic designers, artists, and writers would do their part to create awesome campaigns. I would then present these ideas to the accounts and secure payment. It was a true team effort and if I had to try to do all the parts, it would have been a miserable failure.

Church is the same. There are those who are gifted to speak, do administrative work, pray, serve, and provide hospitality. We all work together to offer a comfortable clean facility with inspiring services, training, children's ministry, youth ministry, and opportunities to serve in the community. It's a true team effort.

I love the story of the ice cream cone. At the 1904 world's fair, Ernest Hamwi was in a booth selling a flat waffle type pastry called Zalabia. Next to Ernest was an ice cream vendor who had plenty of ice cream, but was out of bowls. Earnest came to the rescue by rolling his Zalabia into a cone (referred to as a cornucopia at that time). The cone was then filled with ice cream and handed to the customers. Hamwi later formed the Cornucopia Waffle Company, which later became known as Western Cone Company.

This is another perfect example of partnership!

So, who can you partner with to further the Kingdom?

2. **Multiplies Your Potential** – two horses can pull three times the weight of one horse. It's the same with people. Two people can accomplish more than double what one person can accomplish. My example of the advertising agency is a great example of this. When we work together as a team – many hands make light work – we can increase the potential of each individual.

Have you ever noticed how geese fly in a V formation? The reason they do that is that it adds at least 72% to their flying range. As the front goose gets tired, it will drop to the back, and another will take its place. That's a good lesson for the church. Leaders get tired and need others to help lead. The geese behind the leader honk encouragement. Another good lesson for the church. Everyone should be encouraging the leaders, not complaining and gossiping.

Jesus understood this principle. He didn't try to evangelize the whole world. Instead, he recruited disciples and sent them out 2 x 2. Jesus knew that he could accomplish more in a shorter amount of time, if he had a team.

The results are evident in the millions of Christians around the world.

3. **Recover from Trouble Quicker** – when I think of this principle, I immediately flash to the commercial with the older person who has fallen and can't get up. Every Christian has a time when they fall. Some falls are bigger than others. The key is that we need other believers who come alongside and help us recover.

I helped start Revive40, which is a ministry that helps men recover from sex addiction of various levels. We've discovered that no man is strong enough to recover from this addiction on his own. However, if that man joins with other men who encourage and hold him accountable to living a life of purity, he can get free. This same principle holds true for alcoholics, drug addicts, and those who are overweight.

King Solomon teaches this principle in Ecclesiastes 4:10:

> *"If either of them falls down, one can help the other up. But pity anyone who falls and has no one to help them up."*

I am a huge advocate of small groups. When I first accepted Christ, I was part of a men's small group. We were all new Christians and so we were falling a lot. It was great to have other men to help me recover from trouble, hold me accountable to growing more like Jesus, and pray for me.

4. **Dream Bigger** – I grew up in a church that didn't talk about dreaming or goals or achievement. In fact, I really don't remember much of what they did talk about. So, when I had my chance to break from the church at age 18, I did and didn't go back until I was 40. During my years away from the church, I got involved in personal development and self-help. I learned to dream and dream big. Then, I got saved and all the naysayers started putting down my dreaming. They had good intentions, but it stifled my life for many years. It's only been just recently, in my 60's, that I started dreaming again.

Jesus was a big dreamer. He dreamed of a world where everyone was saved and doing the same works he did. In fact, in John 14:12 (NLT) Jesus said, "I tell you the truth, anyone who believes in me will do the same works I have done, and even greater works, because I am going to be with the Father." Wow! That's a mind-blowing promise that we would do even greater things than he did – resurrection, healing, deliverance, and walking on water. Yet, that's what he said and since he was only saying what the Father said, and God cannot lie, then it must be true.

Through the years, God has given mankind big dreams. If he had not, we would still be living in caves. Think about all the amazing inventions that make our lives better and know that God gave us those ideas. I think often about Thomas Edison who is reported to have failed 10,000 times before inventing the light bulb. I don't know about you, but I'm very thankful for the light bulb. Then there are the Wright brothers who invented the airplane, even though their father, a church leader, said it was impossible.

God gave these men incredible ideas that radically changed our world for the better. Here's the cool part, God is no respecter of persons, so if you are open to receiving them, God will give you big dreams and help you fulfill them.

When I was in high school, God gave me a big dream of writing and publishing books. I had many dream stealers through the years, but I published my first book in 1995 and have published eleven books (including this one) and had two of them translated into German and French. If the Lord allows, I plan to write and publish many more.

What big dream has God given you? What's stopping you from moving forward? Maybe you just need some people who believe in you.

5. **Able to Resist the Devil Better** – if you haven't figured it out, we are in a war. Satan hates us and his sole goal is to steal, kill, and destroy (John 10:10). As we see in Genesis 3, the devil is tricky. He's been around a long time and knows all of our weaknesses, so he knows exactly what will tempt us. When we try to go it alone, we are no match for satan. However, when we have a group of believers around us and are personally seeking the Lord, it's nearly impossible to break us.

Ecclesiastes 4:12 echoes this, "Though one may be overpowered, two can defend themselves. A cord of three strands is not quickly broken."

When we work together with the Lord and other believers, we are like the three-strand cord that is not quickly or easily broken. Jesus himself, didn't try to do ministry by himself. He was surrounded by the twelve disciples and many others who supported his ministry team. If Jesus didn't go solo, why do we think we can?

Get a team of strong believers together. Meet and study God's Word, pray and do ministry together. It will help you stay strong against the temptations of this world.

6. **God Prospers His Partners** – What do you think would happen to your life, if Bill Gates or Jeff Bezos called one day and said he wanted to partner with you? Well, God is a lot richer and more powerful than Gates or Bezos and He is calling you into partnership with Him.

To confirm this, let's examine Psalm 1:1-3 (NLT), "Oh, the joys of those who do not follow the advice of the wicked, or stand around with sinners, or join in with mockers. But they delight in the law of the LORD, meditating on it day and night. They are like trees planted along the riverbank, bearing fruit each season. Their leaves never wither, and they prosper in all they do." (emphasis mine)

We see a great example of this in Luke 5:4-5 (NLT), "When he had finished speaking, he said to Simon, "Now go out where it is deeper, and let down your nets to catch some fish." "Master," Simon replied, "we worked hard all last night and didn't catch a thing. But if you say so, I'll let the nets down again." And this time their nets were so full of fish they began to tear! A shout for help brought their partners in the other boat, and soon both boats were filled with fish and on the verge of sinking."

Here we see Peter having tried on his own unsuccessfully and then partnering with Jesus and other people to enjoy an abundant return. So often we hear that the answer to financial success is to work hard, yet here we see that Peter had worked hard all night. The answer is to work smarter by partnering with God.

Delighting in God's Word and Ways is partnering with Him. When we believe and act on what Malachi said about tithing and giving, we partner with God, and He prospers us.

King Uzziah partnered with God and God prospered him (2 Chronicles 26:5). Abram/Abraham partnered with God (Genesis 12:1-3) and became very wealthy (Genesis 13:2). David partnered with God (1 Samuel 16:13) and died a very wealthy man (1 Chronicles 29:28). Solomon partnered with God (1 Kings 3:5) and became possibly the wealthiest man in the history of the earth (1 Kings 3:10-13). Jesus partnered with the Father and during his three-year ministry, he and none of his disciples had jobs, yet there was always more than enough money.

Isn't it time to partner with God and let Him prosper you and your family?

Next, let's examine the keys to partnering with God:

1. Look for where God is working -

In John 5:17, Jesus said, "My Father is always working, and so am I." God is always at work, we just have to ask Him to show us where He is working, so we can join in.

The problem is that we are always asking God to bless our plans. We get ideas and ask God to give us wisdom and favor in them, but they aren't His plans. He will let us move forward with our plans and we may enjoy some success, but nothing near what would have happened if we were in His plan. Ultimately, God will bring us around to His plan and purpose (Proverbs 19:21).

Where is God working? Wherever there are people in need of salvation, rescuing, teaching, food, water, clothing, shelter, or love. Ask God to open your spiritual eyes and then look around. Also, take note of what moves you emotionally.

How do you feel when you hear a story about a homeless person, struggling single mother or widow, kids who don't have a permanent home or are bouncing around the foster system, sex trafficking, people who are dying of starvation or from tainted water? God is waiting for people like you to help.

Do you love to share the gospel with other people or equip the saints through biblical teaching? How about teaching kids in children's ministry? Maybe you are good with your hands and could help build things for the Kingdom? God is waiting for you too!

God is looking for people He can partner with in His work.

2. Listen for God's still small voice in your spirit -

Isaiah 30:21 (NLT) says, "Your own ears will hear him. Right behind you a voice will say, 'This is the way you should go,' whether to the right or to the left."

Jesus often went off by himself to pray and hear from God. He told the disciples that he did nothing that he hadn't already seen the Father do. Jesus also told them that he said nothing but what he first heard the Father say. In other words, Jesus did nothing and said nothing on his own.

If the Lord Jesus, the Son of God didn't do anything or say anything without first checking in with Father God, shouldn't we be more like that?

3. Be obedient -

It's one thing to listen for God's voice and something completely different to do what He says. People often ask for God to speak and then when He says something completely different from what they were expecting, they think that must not have been God. I recommend listening and obeying, even if you don't agree.

Earlier in the book, I mentioned that in the year 2000, we were $120,000 in debt and asked God for wisdom. He told us to sell our family home. We loved the home, had done a lot of work to make it a perfect fit for our family. It would have been really easy to think that it wasn't God. Instead, we obeyed and sold our home. He told us to do many other things and we were obedient in every case. By 2005 we were debt free.

As you move along the path of God's financial plan, He will ask you to give up things you enjoy. He once asked us to give up TV, movies, and other forms of entertainment for six months. It wasn't fun, but we saved a lot of money and learned other ways to entertain ourselves and our family.

God's plan may be different than our plan, but it is always better and typically results in some type of abundance. In Genesis 12:1, God told Abram (who later became Abraham) to leave his country, people, and family. Abram was obedient and was abundantly blessed.

Ask God for wisdom in your finances, then listen and obey.

4. Let God strengthen you daily -

As He did with so many Bible characters, God will stretch our faith by pushing us out of our comfort zones. There will be new jobs, businesses, inventions, and financial opportunities. He may ask you to sell your home and move to another state or country.

Let God strengthen your faith daily through the Word. Romans 10:17 (NIV) says, "Consequently, faith comes from hearing the message, and the message is heard through the word about Christ." Devote time every day in the Word of God.

Since I was about 16 years old, I've been a weightlifter. Even now, at age 67, I lift three times per week. I've learned that if you want to build muscle you have to tear the muscle down with heavier weights. It's the same with faith, you must use your faith in order to grow it. The more you challenge yourself, the stronger your faith will be.

2 Chronicles 16:9 (NLT) teaches us that, "The eyes of the LORD search the whole earth in order to strengthen those whose hearts are fully committed to him."

As you read and meditate in the Word of God, He will strengthen you for the challenging times ahead, so you can accomplish the good works He has for you, that will result in improvements in your finances and in furthering the Kingdom.

5. Don't limit God -

This seems like a strange concept. How could anyone limit our limitless God? It's easy and we do it all the time. We try to put God in our little boxes, so He fits our plans. He wants to break out and do amazing things, but He won't go against our will.

Isaiah 55:9 teaches us that God's ways are higher than our ways. His plans are better than ours. As I'm writing this, it's early in 2022 and we are finally recovering from the Covid-19 pandemic. In 2020 all the churches were forced to close. There were no stadium or hotel meetings. Everything was done virtually. For many years, we had put God into our boxes for how church should look or how to do evangelism or equipping the saints. We all discovered that God has bigger, better ideas. Now, because of the pandemic, most churches are livestreaming their services and have larger online communities. In the long run the pandemic helped spread the gospel. What we thought was limiting us, was actually expanding us.

One great example of that expansion is what happened with a friend who does quarterly conferences in hotels. The typical attendance is 300 to 500 people. He had a conference scheduled in March, but because of the Corona virus, they couldn't meet in a hotel. He and his team prayed and received wisdom on how to do the event virtually and for free. Instead of 300 to 500 people attending, they had over 30,000 people attend from all around the world. Thousands received Christ and were healed during this multiple day virtual event.

Think about it; you are partnering with the Creator of the universe. How amazing is that? Peter, Andrew, John, and James were all professional fishermen. God called them to leave their businesses to partner with Him to fish for men, and they changed the world!

6. Be a good giver and receiver -

Throughout my business career, I've had several partnerships. They require giving and receiving. God is the original giver and receiver. He gave His Son, so we could receive salvation and be in right relationship with God. He gave His love, so we could love Him and others. God gives us time, talents, and money, so we can bring glory to Him by building the Kingdom here on earth.

I've discovered that I'm a good giver, but had to work on receiving. How about you? It feels great to give and help someone else, but for some reason when we're on the receiving end it's uncomfortable. If you want to enjoy Gods abundant life, that must change. You have to become as good a receiver as you are a giver, otherwise, God won't be able to get the provision to you.

We also must become good receivers when other people give us things. If we aren't good receivers, we are stealing two blessings – the person trying to give you something and your own.

I love the story of the little girl who had a small, ragged teddy bear that she loved. Her father comes to her and says he has something better for her. Behind his back (out of sight of the little girl) is a big, new teddy bear. She doesn't want to give up the bear she loves and misses out on the blessing of a big new teddy bear.

How often have we done that? We hold tightly to what we have, and God wants to give us something bigger and better. We should always hold what we have lightly and be willing to give, so that we can receive God's blessings.

God is the best partner you could ever have. He owns the whole universe, and He wants to partner with you. All you have to do is say, "YES"!

CHAPTER THREE: ACTIVATION

Personal Activities

1. Other than God, make a list of people you are partnering with to do Kingdom work.
2. Now, take that list and identify which of the 4 stages of partnership, referenced in the chapter, you are in with each person on your list from #1.
3. Next, list what you can do to move each one to a higher stage.

Small Group Discussion Questions

1. According to Ecclesiastes, why are two better than one?
2. What are the four stages of partnership and how have you seen those in action in your life?
3. What are the 5 benefits of partnering with God listed in this lesson?

CHAPTER FOUR:
SOWING AND REAPING

In this chapter we're going to dig into the law of sowing and reaping. This is both a natural and spiritual law. It works all the time; you just have to know how to work within the law to produce an abundant harvest.

I remember when I was a kid, we had a small patch of land in our back yard that was designated as a garden. Each spring we would go out and prepare the soil, plant the seeds, and water. I would go out every day to see if anything had grown. I was often temped to dig up the seeds to see what was happening, but was warned by my parents not to do that. Finally, one day there was a little sprout. Eventually we had corn, carrots, beans, watermelon, and cantaloupe. The cool part was that it worked every year exactly the same way.

The keys to sowing and reaping are to prepare the ground, sow the seeds, water, weed, and wait.

Farmers have been doing this for thousands of years. They know exactly how to tap into the law of sowing and reaping for a harvest. But, what would you think of a farmer who bought bags of seed, placed them in his barn, and then waited for a harvest? The farmer is crazy, right? Yet, that is what many Christians are doing. They aren't planting the seed that God gives them, so He can't provide them with a harvest. If you have a job or business and you get paid, but you aren't tithing and giving, then you are like the farmer who doesn't plant his seed and your result will be the same – no harvest.

We see the principle of sowing and reaping throughout the Bible. Let's look at Genesis 1:11:

> *"Then God said, "Let the land produce vegetation: seed-bearing plants and trees on the land that bear fruit with seed in it, according to their various kinds."*

As we see in the scripture, God created the natural law of sowing and reaping on the third day of creation, and it has been in operation ever since. Now, let's shift from the natural law to the spiritual law, which works the same way. Actually, natural laws always come from spiritual laws. The spirit realm existed before the natural realm. Those seed-bearing plants and trees, in Genesis 1:11, existed in the spirit before God brought them to the natural earth.

There are many applications of the spiritual law of sowing and reaping. It works in every aspect of life. If you are seeking love, sow love. If you want more friends, sow friendship. If you want to succeed in your job or business, sow hard and smart work. I think you are probably getting the point. Since we are talking about God's financial plan, let's look at how the spiritual law of sowing and reaping relates to money.

The Apostle Paul wrote extensively about sowing and reaping in 2 Corinthians 9, so let's study the scripture together. In the first five verses Paul is referencing the generosity of the Macedonians (mentioned in 2 Corinthians 8). I think he was creating a little competition between the Macedonians and the Corinthians to see who could be more generous to the Lord. Obviously, we don't give to be better than someone else, but a little competition isn't bad.

In verse 6, Paul gives the key to the law of sowing and reaping. This works whether you are planting natural seeds to grow crops, flowers, bushes, or trees. It also works when you sow spiritual seed, in this case the seed is money, because Paul is talking about a financial offering. Okay, let's read 2 Corinthians 9:6:

> *"Remember this: Whoever sows sparingly will also reap sparingly, and whoever sows generously will also reap generously."*

In God's financial plan, if you sow your financial seed sparingly, you will reap or receive sparingly, but if you sow generously, you will also reap generously. In plain terms, the more you give, the more you will receive. Now, there are some heart issues involved and we see those in verse 7:

> *"Each of you should give what you have decided in your heart to give, not reluctantly or under compulsion, for God loves a cheerful giver."*

I have met people who were abundant givers. In fact, they gave it all and they didn't understand why they were in a constant financial struggle. The first reason is found in verse 7 that we just read. God will put amounts of money on our heart that we are to give. When we give it's out of a cheerful heart, not out of compulsion or greed or trying to manipulate God or trying to look more spiritual or holier than others. We also shouldn't give if we feel like if we don't give, God won't bless or love us. These ungodly motives will stop the harvest. We are to give only the amount God puts on our heart and do it cheerfully, if we want the law of sowing and reaping to work.

There is another piece to this, which we see in verse 10:

> *"Now he who supplies seed to the sower and bread for food will also supply and increase your store of*

*seed and will enlarge the harvest of
your righteousness."*

Here we see that God is the supplier of our money
seed. Some of the money He gives us is for food
and to take care of our needs. The rest is for
planting in order to receive a harvest. The good
news is that if we are good stewards of the money
God gives us, He will continue giving us more
financial seed to sow, which will result in an ever-
increasing harvest.

Karen and I have experienced this. As we learned
about God's financial plan and began to be better
stewards of the money God had given us, we were
able to tithe and give more above the tithe. As we
did that, He caused our business to prosper or
increased commissions in a sales job. Because of
the law of sowing and reaping, our income, in our
60's has been higher than at any other point in our
adult lives. Praise God! He supplies the seed, and
we sow it.

We also reaped in different ways. For example,
when we bought our current house a few years ago,
we found a program that allowed us to buy the
house with a low interest rate and because the
government and the owners of the house gave us
money to cover closing costs, we paid no money out
of our pocket. It's now worth double what we paid.
Another example is when we went to buy our
current car. We found the car we liked and began to
negotiate. God blessed us with a great price, no

money down, and a 0% interest loan. This and the previous example are part of the harvest from seeds planted in past months and years.

Next, let's examine the process for sowing and reaping. First, in order to engage God's system, we must give Him back what He asks for in Malachi 3:10. This is the tithe. 10% of your gross income or any increase. We will dig deeper into the tithe in the next chapter.

After we are tithing, the next step is to prepare the ground of our heart. Just like a farmer must prepare the physical ground before planting, we must do the same thing in the spirit. We do that by reading, studying, meditating, and memorizing the Word of God. This is how we gain understanding of how God's plan works: by increasing our cheerfulness and generosity. Now, don't misread this and think that you don't have to give until your heart is totally ready. The truth is that as long as you live here on earth, it will never be completely ready. You just need to accept that the law of sowing and reaping works and trust God as your provider.

The next step is to seek God for how much of the remaining 90% is for giving. Remember back in 2 Corinthians 9:7 it said that we were to give what we had decided in our heart to give. If we are seeking God, He will give us an amount. Whenever we have an opportunity to give, Karen and I will ask God for an amount and then we will compare. Most often, He will give us the same amount. However, at times we will have two amounts. This just happened to us as we were watching a virtual conference. The figure I got was $500, but Karen got $1000. As I mentioned previously, we've discovered that the larger figure is usually God, because He wants us to get the maximum harvest. We gave $1000 with cheerful hearts.

Now, it's important that we don't either eat the seed that was meant for sowing or give the seed that was meant for eating. In other words, God has provided a certain amount of money for our needs. Now, if we go overboard and live beyond our means, we will be eating our giving seed. So, a huge key to enjoying the benefits of God's financial plan is to keep our living expenses to a minimum. That way we have more financial seed to sow and can enjoy a more abundant harvest.

You can trust that God will always take care of your needs. Philippians 4:19 tells us that God will provide for our needs from His glorious riches. We have a rich Daddy, so no need to worry about finances. Just do your part in seeking wisdom and keeping the living expenses as low as possible and God will take care of the rest. It's when we use credit to spend money, we don't have that we get into trouble. If you've already done that (like so many of us have), we will soon examine some ways Karen and I used to get out of debt.

The next step in the sowing and reaping process is not to keep digging up our seed through doubt or unbelief. Remember, I talked about being a kid and we planted a garden every year. I was impatient and wanted to dig up the seeds to see if they were growing. My parents made sure that I understood that would kill them. Your doubt or unbelief will also kill your financial seed. Remember that Jesus could only do a few miracles in his hometown because of their unbelief. Peter walked on water, but sank because of his doubt. Your harvest is based on your faith in God's system.

Back in 1998, we were living in Tacoma, WA and I was in contact with a young Christian guy in British Columbia, Canada. He was struggling with his faith regarding money. I invited him to come to our church for a men's conference we were hosting and told him he could stay at our house, and we would feed him. He came. During the conference, they did an offering and encouraged guys to sow and trust God for a quick harvest. My friend sowed all the money he had into the offering, which meant he didn't have gas money to get back home. None of us knew this. Later that night he shared with us that the rest of the conference men kept coming up to him and handing him wads of cash, saying that God said to give this to him. My friend ended up with five times what he put in the offering. That's a miraculous and instant harvest. Because of that faith building experience, he is now a very successful businessman.

This was a great example of an instant harvest, which happens at times in God's harvest field. However, most of the time the harvest will take some time and that's where your faith comes in. Do you trust God to provide the harvest?

Next, we are going to discuss the seven keys to the law of sowing and reaping:

1. **We Will Always Reap from What We Sow -**
   Once again, this holds true in every area of your life. If you have financial struggles, it could be because you have sown your money seed into worldly things to satisfy your fleshly desires. Many people use credit cards to buy things they can't afford. Again, we will address some ways to get out of debt in chapter seven, but for right now, if you lack self-control, you need to put the credit cards away and only use cash or your debit card to buy things.

   Let's look at Galatians 6:7-8 (NLT) to see what God has to say about this:

   > *"Don't be misled—you cannot mock the justice of God. You will always harvest what you plant. Those who live only to satisfy their own sinful nature will harvest decay and death from that sinful nature. But those who live to please the Spirit will harvest everlasting life from the Spirit."*

When we sow into worldly things, we are mocking God and we will reap a harvest of consequences. For example, often when we buy things with credit cards, because we can't afford them, we sow into the consequences of debt, high interest charges, and stress. All the prayer in the world, won't get God to eliminate that debt. He needs you to learn a lesson. That said, He will give you wisdom on how to get out of debt quickly. More on that later. The good news is that if we sow to please the Spirit, we will enjoy an everlasting harvest. In other words, God will give us a harvest here on earth and we will store up treasures in heaven!

Now, I want to make it clear that credit, like money, is not good or bad, it's how you use it that determines the results. For example, most of us don't have the cash to buy a house, so we have a mortgage. As long as the mortgage is not more than you can afford, it's a great way to buy a house and as you operate in God's financial plan, He will give you creative ways to pay that mortgage off quicker.

Credit cards are not good or bad (unless you lack self-control and then they are bad). When Karen and I were massively in debt, we had to put the credit cards away and then close the accounts once we paid them off. After God taught us how to use money, we were able to gain benefits from a credit card. For example, we have a Southwest Airlines card that we use to buy most things, but we only buy what we have cash for, and we pay the card balance off every week. The benefit is that we get points to fly, and it allows us to fly places for free every year. That's wisdom from the Lord.

When we live within our means, tithe, and give, we sow into a spiritual harvest in this life and the life to come.

2. **We Reap the Same Kind as We Sow -**
If you sow corn seeds you get corn. Apple seeds result in apples. God has created a system that reproduces its own kind. We see that in the last part of Genesis 1:11:

> *"These seeds will then produce the kinds of plants and trees from which they came."*

Seeds produce their own kind.

In 2 Corinthians 9, the Apostle Paul is talking about a monetary collection for the Christians in Jerusalem. In verse 6, he talks about sowing seeds. Because he is talking about an offering, clearly Paul is talking about money seeds. In verse 10, he says that God is the one who provides these seeds. God is our provider, and He provides some seed to sow (give) and some to use for our personal needs. When we sow money seeds into good ground (church or ministry that is reaching the lost, feeding the hungry, taking care of the poor, etc.), then the harvest will be a money crop.

3. **We Reap in a Different Season Than We Sow**

If you are a farmer, in the proper season, you prepare the soil, sow the seeds, and wait for the harvest. A farmer who expected a harvest the day after planting would be crazy. It takes time for the seed to grow and produce a harvest.

Jesus taught about this in Mark 4:27-29 (NLT):

> *"Night and day, while he's asleep or awake, the seed sprouts and grows, but he does not understand how it happens. The earth produces the crops on its own. First a leaf blade pushes through, then the heads of wheat are formed, and finally the grain ripens. And as soon as the grain is ready, the farmer comes and harvests it with a sickle, for the harvest time has come."*

The sowing and reaping principles work with any type of sowing. You sow your financial seeds in one season and in most cases the harvest will come in a different season. The good news is that sometimes that season is a few hours or a day. On the other hands, sometimes that season is several years. Fortunately, God is always faithful and there will be a harvest.

Sowing and reaping often requires us to exercise the fruit of patience and your faith in God as provider. James 5:7-8 (NLT) teaches this:

> *"Dear brothers and sisters, be patient as you wait for the Lord's return. Consider the farmers who patiently wait for the rains in the fall and in the spring. They eagerly look for the valuable harvest to ripen. You, too, must be patient. Take courage, for the coming of the Lord is near."*

4. **We Reap More Than What We Sow -**
I have not been able to discover an exact science to God's sowing and reaping system, but I do know that it works, and it always produces more than what you sow. For example, if you sow one corn seed, you get a stalk with many ears, each with many individual corn kernels.

In Matthew 14:13-21 we see God's multiplication system at work, as Jesus feeds 5,000 men, plus women and children (possibly 15,000 to 20,000 people) with five loaves (probably like a pita) and two fish (probably small smoked fish). This was meant to feed a young boy, not a multitude, but when it's in the hands of the Provider, it multiplies. God takes the financial seeds sown and multiplies them back to us.

This principle works even during bad financial times. In Genesis 26 there is a severe famine. Isaac (son of Abraham) was going to move to Egypt (where there was food), but God told him to stay in his land and sow. Isaac obeyed. Let's see what happened:

Genesis 26:12 (NLT):

> *"When Isaac planted his crops that year, he harvested a hundred times more grain than he planted, for the LORD blessed him."*

There is an old saying that you can't out give God and I'll give personal testimony to that in my life. I have always received back way more than I give.

5. We Reap in Proportion to What We Sow - This seems to be a contradiction of the 4th principle, but it isn't. Let me explain. God will always produce a harvest bigger than what we sow, but how much we sow also dictates the size of the harvest.

Back to 2 Corinthians 9:6:

> "Remember this: Whoever sows sparingly will also reap sparingly, and whoever sows generously will also reap generously."

Earlier in the book, I told the story of the good king and his party. Everyone was invited to bring water and at the end of the party they each could take as much treasure as would fit into their water container. Those who gave more water received more treasure.

Jesus teaches this in Luke 6:38 (NLT):

> *"Give, and you will receive. Your gift will return to you in full— pressed down, shaken together to make room for more, running over, and poured into your lap. The amount you give will determine the amount you get back."*

The amount you give is then multiplied by God and you receive a bigger harvest. The more you give, the more you get back.

D.H Lawrence is reported to have said:

If you want to be rich ... GIVE!
If you want to be poor ... GRASP!
If you want abundance ... SCATTER!
If you want to be needy . . HOARD!

If you are generous with God, He will be even more generous with you. Many times, we have given a $100 offering and received $1,000 or more back. That takes $100 faith. Giving $100 was easy, but one time God told us to give $1,000. Wow, that was a lot of money, but since He had been faithful with the $100 gifts, we figured He would be faithful with $1,000 and He was.

Where is your giving faith level? Maybe it's time to bump it up.

6. **We Reap a Full Harvest Only If We Persevere -**
The farmer only reaps a full harvest if he waits patiently until the harvest is ready. If he were to go out and harvest early, his crop wouldn't ripen and be fully grown; it's the same with our financial sowing.

Galatians 6:9-10:

> *"Let us not become weary in doing good, for at the proper time we will reap a harvest if we do not give up. Therefore, as we have opportunity, let us do good to all people, especially to those who belong to the family of believers."*

There will be times when you give, and you must persevere to get to the harvest. If you begin to doubt or give up on God, your crop will die. Keep believing, until the harvest comes in.

At the end of the parable of the sower (Matthew 13:1-8, which is about sowing the Word of God for salvation), Jesus says, "Still other seed fell on good soil. It came up, grew and produced a crop, some multiplying thirty, some sixty, some a hundred times."

I believe that God has shown me that this has application when sowing money seed, as well. The rate of return depends on how long you are willing to persevere in faith. Do you have 30, 60, or 100-fold faith?

7. We Can't Do Anything About Last Year's Harvest, So Forget About It -

I really dislike it when people say, "you should have" to me. My response is always "I can't should have anything". That's in the past and I have no control over it. I can learn from the past, but I'm focused on the now and looking to the future.

Isaiah 43:18 says:

> *"Forget the former things; do not dwell on the past."*

In Philippians 3:13-14, Paul echoes this concept:

> *"...but one thing I do: forgetting what lies behind and reaching forward to what lies ahead, I press on toward the goal for the prize..."* (emphasis mine)

We can't do anything about the failures last year, month, day, hour, or minute. All we can affect is what we do right now, in this moment and the next and the next.

One principle will always be true. If you didn't have a good financial year or month, you need to sow less into the world and more into the Kingdom of God.

CHAPTER FOUR: ACTIVATION

Personal Activities

1. Make a list of times you have sowed and reaped more than you sowed. Use this to increase your faith for sowing and reaping.
2. If you have had some bad financial years, put those behind you, begin the process of sowing and reaping fresh and new.
3. Beyond your regular tithe and giving, find a need at your church, a person or ministry in need, and begin giving to them.
4. Keep a record of what you give. Then watch for, and make note of, the harvest.
5. If that giving opportunity ends, find another. Make it a continuous part of your giving.

Small Group Discussion Questions

1. According to the lesson, where do we first see the law of sowing and reaping in action?
2. God supplies financial seed for two purposes; what are they?
3. What are the six parts to the process of sowing and reaping? Where would you say you are in the process?

CHAPTER FIVE:
TITHING

In previous chapters I've mentioned the importance of tithing. In this chapter we are going to dig deep into tithing and whether New Testament believers should tithe. First, I want to say that I don't believe that New Testament Christians are required to tithe. Rather, we are given the opportunity to tithe. In fact, since grace is so much bigger and better than the law, tithing should be the least amount of money that New Testament Christians give.

The reality is that God isn't going to force us to tithe. He's given us free will and that applies to the tithe. However, it's important for us to have all the facts when we try to make a decision. So, let's look at some of the facts about tithing from Malachi 3:8-12:

> *"'Will a mere mortal rob God? Yet you rob me.' But you ask, 'How are*

we robbing you?' 'In tithes and offerings. You are under a curse—your whole nation—because you are robbing me. Bring the whole tithe into the storehouse, that there may be food in my house. Test me in this,' says the LORD Almighty, 'and see if I will not throw open the floodgates of heaven and pour out so much blessing that there will not be room enough to store it. I will prevent pests from devouring your crops, and the vines in your fields will not drop their fruit before it is ripe,' says the LORD Almighty. 'Then all the nations will call you blessed, for yours will be a delightful land,' says the LORD Almighty."

Back in 2000, when we were $120,000 in debt, we were robbing God. In hindsight, it's no wonder we were so far in debt. One piece of wisdom that God taught us was to quit robbing Him and start tithing. It was the activator for His financial plan. From the moment we began tithing until today, we have never lacked or been back in debt. Tithing works!

Let's go back to basics and talk about what is a tithe? I do this because I've encountered a number of people who told me they were tithing 5% or 8% or a certain dollar amount every month. That's not tithing. The Hebrew word translated as tithe is *maaser*, which means a tenth part or payment of a tenth part. So, a tithe is 10%, but that begs the question, 10% of what?

As I mentioned previously, Psalm 24:1 teaches us that everything belongs to the Lord. That means all the money we receive actually belongs to Him. We are just stewards or caretakers of His money. The good news is that even though it's all His money, He let us keep 90% of it to use as we see fit. All He asks is that we give Him His 10%. I've been in business for many years and had a few partnerships. I've never had a partner who said I could have 90% of the profit while they just took 10%. Yet, that is exactly what God is doing. It's an amazing partnership, as long as we hold up our part of the deal.

So, the tithe is 10% of all the money we receive. Whenever I teach this, there is always someone who asks if it's 10% of the gross or net? In other words, they are asking if it's 10% of the 100% (before taxes, medical, 401k, etc.) and the answer is YES! If it all belongs to God, then the tithe would be 10% of the gross amount we receive. Before you start groaning, remember that you get to keep the other 90% and, in God's system, the 90% will go further than the 100%.

The tithe is also a first fruits offering, which means God wants it first, before you go out to dinner or a movie or pay your bills. He wants you to trust Him as provider. Tithing is really about obedience and trust in God. He doesn't need our money, but He does need our whole heart.

God gave His first and only Son, Jesus, so that he could be the first of many brothers and sisters to enter into the Kingdom of God. Jesus was an example of a first fruits offering. Personally, I'm thankful for God's tithe, as it opened the door for financial blessings.

The reason God wants the tithe paid first, is so you will trust Him to provide for everything else. Unfortunately, most Christians have it backwards. They intend to tithe, but after paying all the bills, there isn't much left over. Imagine how you would feel if all your creditors are lined up in a row and God is the last one. You go along and pay each one what you owe. Then, you get to God - the one who loves you; the one who created you; the one who died for you, and there is no money left over. How would you feel standing there looking in God's eyes with nothing to give Him?

By my experience and many others, I've interviewed, if you pay the tithe first, God will provide for all the rest. Plus, if you aren't paying your tithe, you are stealing from God. Remember, it's all His money and He has only asked for 10%. That 10% doesn't belong to you, so if you spend it, you are robbing God.

The Israelites were doing exactly that, and God dealt with them through the prophet Malachi. Let's look at Malachi 3:8-9 again:

> *"Will a mere mortal rob God? Yet you rob me. "But you ask, 'How are we robbing you?' "In tithes and offerings. You are under a curse— your whole nation—because you are robbing me."*

Now, God mentions the tithe and offering. We will study the offering in the next chapter. For now, we will deal only with the tithe. The scripture is clear, if you are not tithing you are robbing God. Again, I'm going to say that we aren't required to tithe, we get to tithe, and I don't know about you, but I certainly don't want to be known as a God-robber.

Let me show you an illustration that should drive this point home. If I borrowed $20 from my friend Skip, I now have $20 in my possession. Who does that $20 belong to? It's in my possession, but it belongs to Skip. He loaned it to me. If I go and spend that $20 on my own needs and never pay him back, I stole that money. Now, Skip is a good friend, and he would probably forgive me, but he would certainly hesitate to loan money to me again. If we show God that we are not faithful with the tithe, He's less likely to bless us with more.

Okay, let's address the curse mentioned in Malachi 8. Jesus went to the cross and took the curses with him. He became a curse for us, so there is no longer a curse associated with the tithe. That said, there are always consequences for our actions. If we rob a bank and get caught, we will go to jail. If we rob from God, we miss out on His blessing. We will look at those promised blessings a little later in this chapter.

Let's move on to the first part of Malachi 3:10 to see where we are to pay the tithe:

> *"Bring the whole tithe into the storehouse, that there may be food in my house."*

In the days when Malachi was written, people brought the tithe of their flocks and crops. The temple had a storehouse where all of this was kept. Thankfully we don't bring crops and animals to church. The church would be a messy, stinky place. Instead, we bring money, but the place is still the same. Your local church is the storehouse and the place where you pay your tithe.

Now, you would think that living in one of the wealthiest countries in the world, the percentage of Christians who tithe would be very high. Yet, according to the last Barna Research study, Christians give on average 2.5%, which is down from 3.3% during the Great Depression. Wow! Did you catch that. In the worst time in American financial history Christians were giving more than they are right now. That's very sad and it's why so many churches are struggling to make ends meet. It's also why so many Christians have financial troubles.

I remember listening to a missionary at a church service. He talked about a group of Christians in a very poor country where it wasn't illegal to be a Christian, but it wasn't the religion of the country. The government dictated by law that Christians could only give 2% of their income. This group of Christians was lobbying the government to raise that to at least 10%, so they could tithe. Wow! In a poor country where it is illegal to tithe, they were fighting for the right to tithe. Here in the U.S., where we are free to tithe, Christians are always trying to find loopholes, so they don't have to tithe. Amazing!

One of the biggest loopholes I hear is that the tithe was in the law, and we aren't under the law, we are under grace. This is true and untrue. Yes, the tithe was part of the law, but it also existed long before God gave the law to Moses. Let's examine that in Genesis 14:18-20:

> *"Then Melchizedek king of Salem brought out bread and wine. He was priest of God Most High, and he blessed Abram, saying, "Blessed be Abram by God Most High, Creator of heaven and earth. And praise be to God Most High, who delivered*

your enemies into your hand. Then
Abram gave him a tenth of
everything."

This is the first example of the tithe in the Bible, and it is over 400 years before the law. Let's examine this scripture to see why Abram, who became Abraham, known as the father of faith, gave a tithe to this guy named Melchizedek. Let's first study Melchizedek, and to do that we need to read Hebrews 7:1-4:

"This Melchizedek was king of Salem and priest of God Most High. He met Abraham returning from the defeat of the kings and blessed him, and Abraham gave him a tenth of everything. First, the name Melchizedek means "king of righteousness"; then also, "king of Salem" means "king of peace." Without father or mother, without genealogy, without beginning of days or end of life, resembling the Son of God, he remains a priest forever. Just think how great he was: Even the patriarch Abraham gave him a tenth of the plunder!

So, who do you think Melchizedek was and why did Abram give him a tithe? Well, let's look at the evidence. It says he is the king of Salem. In documented history there was no city called Salem in that area. Jerusalem was at times referred to as Salem and who is the ultimate king of Jerusalem? Jesus. It also says that Melchizedek was a priest of the God most High. The only other person in the Bible who is referenced as a king and priest is Jesus. In the Genesis description, it says that Melchizedek met Abram with bread and wine, which sounds a lot like communion.

In the Hebrews text above, it says that the name Melchizedek means "king of righteousness" and "king of Salem", which means "king of peace". Jesus is the only other person referenced in this way. Lastly, in Hebrews 7:3, it says about Melchizedek, that he was "without father or mother, without genealogy, without beginning of days or end of life, resembling the Son of God". That clearly doesn't describe any human who has ever lived on the earth, but it does describe the Son of God or a pre-incarnate Jesus. No one knows for sure, but many theologians believe this very well could have been the Son of God, in the form of a man.

In any case, Abram was intimate with God and so he recognized divinity. His first response was to pay a tithe. In my thinking, Abram was tithing to the Son of God, just as we New Testament Christians do today. We aren't forced to tithe, it's our reaction to divinity.

Another of the loopholes I hear quite often is that the tithe isn't referenced in the New Testament.

This isn't true. In fact, Jesus mentioned it in Matthew 23:23:

> *"Woe to you, teachers of the law and Pharisees, you hypocrites! You give a tenth of your spices—mint, dill and cumin. But you have neglected the more important matters of the law— justice, mercy and faithfulness. You should have practiced the latter, without neglecting the former."*

Jesus not only mentioned it, but said that it should not be neglected. In other words, we should tithe. Although the Apostle Paul doesn't use the word, it sure sounds like he's describing the tithe in 1 Corinthians 16:2:

> *"On the first day of every week, each one of you should set aside a sum of money in keeping with your income, saving it up, so that when I come no collections will have to be made."*

Imagine if all Christians tithed, no collections would have to be made and all the needs of the church, communities, and world could be met. I don't know about you, but if Abram/Abraham, Jesus, and Paul all thought tithing was correct, why shouldn't we?

Okay, back to Malachi 3:10-12 to see one incredible statement and two amazing promises from God, if we tithe:

> *"'Test me in this,' says the LORD Almighty, 'and see if I will not throw open the floodgates of heaven and pour out so much blessing that there will not be room enough to store it. I will prevent pests from devouring your crops, and the vines in your fields will not drop their fruit before it is ripe,' says the LORD Almighty. 'Then all the nations will call you blessed, for yours will be a delightful land,' says the LORD Almighty."*

Let's break this down. God says, about the tithe, to test him. It's the only place in the Bible where I've found God giving us permission to test Him. Incredible! Next, He gives two promises:

> 1. *"Throw open the floodgates of heaven and pour out so much blessing that there will not be room enough to store it."* Let's start with the floodgates of heaven. The only other place these are mentioned in the Bible is in the account of the flood during Noah's time. That was a lot of water, and this is a lot of blessing. So much blessing we don't have room enough for it all. Wow!

2. "*I will prevent pests from devouring your crops, and the vines in your fields will not drop their fruit before it is ripe.*" What God was saying here is that not only was He going to bless the tither with overflowing blessings, but He would also protect all He had given them. It was very interesting that in our life before we began tithing, things were breaking down regularly and after we started tithing, things rarely broke down. Now, the Bible doesn't promise this, but I think it's part of the blessing that comes from the protection promise in Malachi 3:11.

Those are two amazing promises that are available to those who tithe. It's still your choice as to whether you tithe or not, but considering those promises, I think it's crazy not to tithe. God doesn't want us to tithe to take from us. He wants us to tithe, so He can bless us with more! That's a key piece in His financial plan.

Since the New Testament doesn't say much about tithing, I wondered what the early church fathers had to say on the topic. Here is what I found:

- Irenaeus was Bishop of Lugdunum in Gaul. His writing was formative in the early development of Christian theology. He was a disciple of Polycarp, who was a direct disciple of the Apostle John.

Irenaeus wrote: "Instead of the law enjoining the giving of tithes, to share all our possessions with the poor." He is saying that under the law we should tithe, but under grace we should share everything we have with the poor. Remember when Jesus told the rich young ruler to sell everything and give the money to the poor? It appears that the early church leaders like Irenaeus were saying the same thing.

Here is another of Irenaeus' writings: "And for this reason, they (the Jews) had indeed the tithes of their goods consecrated to Him, but those who have received liberty (grace) set aside all their possessions for the Lord's purposes, bestowing joyfully and freely not the less valuable portions of their property, since they have the hope of better things; as that poor widow acted who cast all her living into the treasury of God." Again, it appears that he is saying that New Testament Christians should give everything for the purposes of God.

- There are a number of other early church fathers who echoed what Irenaeus taught – that the tithe was the very least and we should consider making everything available for the church. We see this in action in Acts 4:32 & 34-35:

"All the believers were one in heart and mind. No one claimed that any of their possessions was their own, but they shared everything they had." And God's grace was so powerfully at work in them all that there were no needy persons among them. For from time to time those who owned land or houses sold them, brought the money from the sales and put it at the apostles' feet, and it was distributed to anyone who had need."

Personally, I think that worldly thinking, greed, and materialism have crept into Christianity. We see it in the "name it, claim it" teachings that have been in the church for many years – give your tithe or offering, name it (Lord, this is for my Mercedes), and God would give it to you. That relegates God to a cosmic Santa Claus and it's not who He is. Also, Christians started acting like people of the world. They use credit cards to live above their means and quit tithing and giving. If that's you, it's time to confess to God and make the necessary changes so you are living debt free, below your means, and both tithing and giving.

Let's do a quick recap. Not tithing is robbing God. That's bad! Tithing allows us to test God, which is exciting. He then promises to give us overflowing blessings and to protect the 90% He allows us to keep. That's very good! At the end of Malachi 3:12 it says that when we tithe, all the nations will call us blessed. That's amazing! The tithe is really the minimum and we should be giving as much as we can, above the tithe, to help the poor and grow the Kingdom on earth. The tithe always goes to the local church where you are being fed the Word of God and are part of the body of Christ. The tithe will then be used to take care of the priests/pastors, cover church operational expenses, and take care of the poor (both inside and outside the church walls). We don't tithe because we have to, we tithe because we love God and choose to!

If everyone who claims to be a Christian were to tithe, there would truly be no lack in the church or local community. In fact, we could probably eliminate homelessness and world hunger and spread the gospel to the entire world. Then Jesus can come back, and we can enjoy eternity. We've got a long way to go, but it must start we each of us!

CHAPTER FIVE: ACTIVATION

Personal Activities

1. If you are not currently tithing (10% of your gross income and increase), then your activation is to begin. Either write the first check or make an electronic payment of 10% of your gross income, to your church, before you pay any other bills or spend any money. Test God in this and see what He does.

2. If you are already tithing, make a list of how He has poured out blessings on you and protected the other 90%.

3. Re-read Hebrews 7:1-4 and compare your attitude about tithing to that of Abraham. If your attitude isn't the same as his, it's time for an attitude adjustment.

Small Group Discussion Questions

1. If you aren't tithing, why? If you are tithing, are you tithing off the gross or net?

2. What are the two benefits of tithing listed in Malachi 3:10-11? If you aren't tithing, are those benefits you are interested in?

3. Why do you think Abram gave Melchizedek a tithe of his increase?

CHAPTER SIX:
GIVING

In Malachi 3:8, God said that the Israelites were robbing Him of tithes and offerings. In the last chapter, I thoroughly covered the tithe. Hopefully there is no doubt in your mind that you should be tithing and have started. In this chapter we are going to talk about the offerings. The offering is when we give anything above the tithe. As I talked about in the last chapter, all our money belongs to God and all He asks for is the tithe (10% of the gross increase and income). He allows us to keep the other 90%. However, He doesn't expect us to spend all the rest of the money on ourselves. He does expect us to use some of it to give offerings.

Giving is part of God's very nature. We see this throughout the Bible. First, He created the universe in such a way that earth could support human life. Then He made mankind and placed them in paradise. He gave us the whole world and all the creatures to steward. When we messed that up, He gave us the law. When we couldn't fulfill the law, He sent His only begotten Son to earth to die for us. That's a true giver and we are made in His image and likeness.

John 3:16 shows this:

> *"For God so loved the world that he gave his one and only Son, that whoever believes in him shall not perish but have eternal life."*

God loved us so much that He did what? Gave His one and only Son! If you are a parent, would you sacrifice one of your children for the homeless guy down the road? How about the child molester or murder on the news? Probably not. Yet, God did. He sacrificed His Son for every person on the planet.

God is the original giver. He gave us this amazing world that sits at the perfect distance from the sun, so we don't burn up or freeze. He gave us gravity, so we don't float off the planet. He gave us oxygen to breathe. We take all these for granted, but without them, we would die. God gave us this amazing world and then He gave us His Son.

Jesus continued in the giving ways of His Father. He gave up the glories of heaven, gave up his godly attributes, and took on human flesh. He then gave three years of his life teaching how we are to live as givers. He gave healing, resurrected life, food, and then gave his own life, so that we could live new lives.

We, God's children, are expected to carry on in the same way, as givers. God expects us to give our time to help others – start with your spouse, children, extended family and then move on to fellow church members, friends, neighbors, co-workers, bosses, and the poor.

God also expects us to give of our talents and giftings. I talked about this in the section on Stewardship. Once you have determined both your natural talents – building, fixing, cooking, writing, speaking, organizing, etc. and your spiritual giftings, then begin to use them to serve the body of Christ and the community.

That said, our focus in this book is on God's financial plan, so in the balance of the chapter I will talk about giving money. Let's begin with some keys to giving that we find in 2 Corinthians 9:6-8. I'm going to show it to you in both the NIV and NLT, as together they help us see the keys:

> *"Remember, the man who plants only a few seeds will not have much grain to gather. The man who plants many seeds will have much grain to gather. Each man should give as he has decided in his heart. He should not give, wishing he could keep it. Or he should not give if he feels he has to give. God loves a man who gives because he wants to give. God can give you all you need. He will give*

you more than enough. You will have everything you need for yourselves. And you will have enough left over to give when there is a need." (NLT)

"Remember this: Whoever sows sparingly will also reap sparingly, and whoever sows generously will also reap generously. [7] Each of you should give what you have decided in your heart to give, not reluctantly or under compulsion, for God loves a cheerful giver. [8] And God is able to bless you abundantly, so that in all things at all times, having all that you need, you will abound in every good work." (NIV)

Seven Keys to Giving:

1. Give Generously -

As I mentioned before, 2 Corinthians 9 is all about an offering, so in verse 6 where Paul talks about sowing generously, he is saying to give generously. Based on the thoughts of early church leaders (in the previous chapter), Paul is really saying, "Give until it hurts or give sacrificially".

This always reminds me of the story of the church that was putting on a special breakfast for the Pastors. The chicken looked at the pig and said, "I could give some eggs and you could give some bacon." The pig responded, "For you that's an offering, but for me it's a complete sacrifice." Jesus gave that type of offering – he gave it all.

So did the widow in Luke 21:1-4:

"As Jesus looked up, he saw the rich putting their gifts into the temple treasury. He also saw a poor widow put in two very small copper coins. 'Truly I tell you,' he said, 'this poor widow has put in more than all the others. All these people gave their gifts out of their wealth; but she out of her poverty put in all she had to live on.'"

We need to adopt that type of a giving heart, as it gives God more opportunity to show His ability to abundantly provide!

2. Give Cheerfully -
2 Corinthians 9:7 tells us that we are to be a cheerful giver. It's not enough just to give; it's all about the motivation and attitude. We are not to give under compulsion. We are not to give reluctantly. If you don't have the heart of a giver, allow God to mold you and begin to give. I think often of the great feeling I have when I give to help someone

who is in need or to fund a Kingdom project. Some of my favorites are feeding the starving children in other countries or providing a water well for a community where they are dying from drinking contaminated water. These both tug at my heart and I will give generously and regularly.

I mentioned earlier in the book that the Greek word translated as cheerful is *hilaros*, which is where we get our word hilarious. God wants us to be hilarious givers. Have you ever watched football fans at a game? They jump up and down, yell, and slap high fives. That's how we should be acting when it's offering time at a church service or conference.

3. **Give What's on Your Heart -**
   2 Corinthians 9:7 also says that we should give what we have decided in our heart to give. Offering time is a very important time in a service, so make sure you pray before you give. Ask God how much you should give (above your tithe). He will put an amount on your heart. If you get two amounts, the larger one is always God, and the lower amount is either the devil or your selfish flesh. Give the higher amount.

In 2000, while we were still deeply in debt, God told us to give $1,500 to my spiritual mentor who was launching a ministry. We gave it cheerfully and in 2004 reaped a $70,000 harvest. That's a much better return than we could have gotten investing the money in the world's system. Now, that doesn't always happen and it hasn't happened since, and we don't give to get. That said, we do plant seeds for future harvests and God likes to give us a bigger harvest than what we planted.

In 2003 we sold some stock and were going to take a trip for our 15th wedding anniversary. The trip was going to take all the money we received from the stock sale. Just as we were getting ready to book the trip, God told us to give $700 to the church to pay for a new glass top stove. We gave it cheerfully and went back to look for cheaper trips, but found our original trip for $700 less. Imagine that!

When we give what He puts on our heart, He will always take care of us.

4. **Give and God will Provide –**
   2 Corinthians 9:8 says that God is able to bless us so abundantly that we will have all we need, and plenty left over to give to every good work. The key is to learn to trust in God as your provider. Let's look at another scripture that we studied earlier in the book, Luke 6:38 (NKJV):

"Give, and it will be given to you: good measure, pressed down, shaken together, and running over will be put into your bosom. For with the same measure that you use, it will be measured back to you."

The Greek word that is translated as "bosom" is *kolpos*, which means a hollow formed by the upper part of a rather loose garment, used for keeping and carrying things. Today, this would be the equivalent of a pocket, wallet, or purse. God is saying that if you give, He will fill your pockets, wallet, or purse with more money, so you can give whenever a need arises.

A few years ago, I was at a church prayer meeting and a man I knew walked up and put something in my pocket. I wondered what it was, but we were having a great time with the Lord and so I waited until after the meeting to check. It was a folded $100 bill. God used that man to put money in my pocket. I have since heard that this has happened to many people. It may happen to you as well, but more likely God will give you favor at work or in your business, which will result in financial increases.

5. **Give Freely -**
    In Matthew 10:8, Jesus gives instructions to the twelve apostles about preaching, teaching, healing, raising the dead, and driving out demons. It's his final comment I want to focus on, "Freely you have received; freely give." God has given freely to us – money, time, talents. It's time for us to give freely.

    Proverbs 11:24 talks about this as well:

    "One person gives freely, yet gains even more; another withholds unduly, but comes to poverty."

    One of my favorite stories of freely giving is about R. G. LeTourneau. He was a Christian businessman who dedicated his life and business to God. From the very beginning, he gave freely, and his business prospered. He is reported to having said, "I shovel out the money, and God shovels it back – but God has a bigger shovel." This goes along with the old saying that you can't outgive God.

    LeTourneau continued to increase his giving percentage and God continued to bless him even more. At one point he was giving 90% of his income to the work of the Lord and living on 10%. That's called reverse tithing. What if you were making a million dollars a year; could you live on $100,000? God is looking for people who that kind of heart, so He can bless them with abundance.

6. **Give Your Best -**
The Bible is full of stories of God blessing people who gave their best. In Genesis 4:3-5, we find the story of Cain and Abel bringing offerings to the Lord. Abel brings the best of his flocks, but Cain brings some of the leftovers from his crops. The Lord looked with favor on Abel's offering and accepted it, but He did not look with favor at Cain's offering and rejected it.

The widow in Mark 12:41-45 gave her best. In fact, she gave everything she had, because she knew God was a good provider and would take care of her. Jesus saw her do this and told the disciples that she had given more than all the rich people.

Giving your best may hurt some at first. It may force you out of your comfort zone. I remember hearing a pastor talk about a time early in his walk when the Lord told him to give $1000. He told the Lord that was all he had in the bank. He felt like the Lord said, "that's why I didn't ask you to give more."

When we give our best, we honor God, so always give your best and give it first. God will look upon it with favor and bless you back!

7. Give in Secret -

In Matthew 6:1-4, Jesus teaches that we aren't supposed to make a big deal about our giving. The religious leaders and wealthy were making the offering a show of how much they were giving, so people would be impressed. When you give, don't let anyone else know the amount (of course your spouse can know). It's all about you and God.

Now, this doesn't mean other people can't see you giving. Just don't make a big deal or talk about how much you are giving. It's good for people to see others giving, as it helps to increase their faith.

One of my favorite secret giving moments (I guess it won't be secret now) was a few years ago at Christmas time. I was working out at a gym several days a week and there was a woman who cleaned the machines. She always had a smile on her face and was meticulous about her cleaning. I appreciated the good work she was doing, and several times told her thanks for doing such a great job.

We were blessed with a financial bonus and as I was praying about how to give (again above the tithe). The woman at the gym came to mind and an amount. I got that amount of cash (which was a large amount) and placed it in a Christmas card. I didn't know her name, so I gave it to the front counter and explained who it was for and asked that they not let her know who had given it. They later told me that she cried when she opened the envelope and said it was an answer to prayer.

Look around and listen for God's direction. You will find all kinds of fun ways to give in secret and bless people!

Those are the seven keys to giving. To wrap up this chapter, I want to talk about another type of giving – Alms. Luke 12:33 (NKJV) mentions this type of giving:

> *"Sell what you have and give alms; provide yourselves money bags which do not grow old, a treasure in the heavens that does not fail, where no thief approaches nor moth destroys."*

Alms is giving specifically to the poor. In Acts 10:4 an angel appears to Cornelius (a Gentile Centurion) and tells him that his prayers and alms have come before God. That resulted in God sending Peter and Cornelius' entire family was saved. When you do your monthly or weekly budget (more on this in the next chapter), set aside some money for alms. Get cash and place it in an envelope in your car or purse. Ask God to show you the people He wants you to bless. Seek to give all of the money each week or month and over time, as God blesses you, increase the amount.

I recently read this and liked it. There are three types of givers:

Flint – you hammer on them, but you just get sparks.
Sponge – you have to squeeze them to get anything.
Honeycomb – they overflow with sweet giving.

Which type of giver are you now? Which would you like to be?

I'd like to finish this chapter with one of my favorite giving stories. The following is reported as a true story, witnessed by Rev. Robert Costa. In 1984, Mike and his family belonged to an East Coast church. One Sunday evening, the sermon was on sacrificial offerings, and a special offering was taken at the end of the sermon. The only money in Mike's wallet was a $50 bill, which was supposed to buy a week's worth of groceries for his wife, their five children, and himself. However, in a move of faith, Mike put the $50 bill in the offering.

After the conclusion of the service, the family went out to the parking lot to go home. Within minutes, they joyfully returned to the sanctuary, and asked the pastor to come outside and see their miracle. Somewhat skeptical, the pastor accompanied them outside to their 20-year-old station wagon. Peering through the windows, he saw that the interior of the vehicle was completely filled with bags of groceries. Happy for the family, he remarked that someone had given them a huge blessing. "You don't understand, pastor," Mike said. "Before service, I made sure that all the windows were rolled up and the doors were locked. I have the only key, so it must have been the Lord!" To which the pastor added, "Giving truly is the only key to God's provision!" (Mike had no family living in the area, and no one from the congregation ever claimed responsibility.)

We are made in God's image and likeness to be givers. It's our selfish flesh that hinders our giving and the abundant blessings God would like to overflow into our lives. All we have to do is become a cheerful and generous giver. I challenge you in the next year to set an audacious and seemingly impossible giving goal and watch what God does.

CHAPTER SIX: ACTIVATION

Personal Activities

1. Evaluate your current giving (above the tithe) and decide if you are a generous giver. If not, increase your giving until you are.
2. The next time you are at a church service or faced with an opportunity to give to a ministry, ask God what you should give. If you get two amounts, the larger one is God; give that amount.
3. Look at the time you are giving to the Lord. Would you say you are giving freely? If not, then find some other ways you can give your time to serving the Lord.
4. One of the keys to giving is to give in secret. Ask around for someone in your church body who is in financial need and give a large gift (at least $100) secretly to them.

Small Group Discussion Questions

1. Since the tithe belongs to God, what is giving?
2. Why are we to be givers?
3. What are the 7 keys to giving that are listed in this lesson and how are you doing with each of those?

CHAPTER SEVEN:
DEBT ELIMINATION

As I've mentioned a couple times earlier in the book, in 2000 we were $120,000 in debt, not including our mortgage. In this chapter, I'm going to share some of the wisdom God gave us that resulted in us being debt free five years later.

The first key to debt freedom and financial increase is to believe that God wants you prosperous and not in debt. Jeremiah 29:11 (NIV) gives us that assurance:

> *"For I know the plans I have for you," declares the LORD, "plans to prosper you and not to harm you, plans to give you hope and a future."*

I briefly addressed this in the introduction, but want to go a little deeper here. The NIV is one of the few translations that uses the word "prosper" and when I study the original Hebrew word, in my opinion, prosper is the best translation. Let's take a moment to examine that. It helped me gain assurance that God loved us and wants us to prosper. I hope it does the same for you.

First, let's define prosper. Merriam-Webster dictionary defines prosper as, "to achieve economic success and to become strong and flourishing. Prosperity is not all about money. Money is part of it, but it's about every aspect of your life flourishing.

Now, we examined this earlier, but it's worth another look at the Hebrew word that is translated as prosper in Jeremiah 29:11. As you may remember, it's the word *Shalowm*, which we most often see defined as peace. Peace is a good definition, but not complete. Strong's Concordance defines *Shalowm* as, completeness, which means that nothing is missing. That means nothing is missing in your health, relationships, well-being, and finances. As the definitions drill down in the Strong's, we find prosperity. If we think of prosperity as more than money, we get the completeness that was intended. Plus, if nothing is missing in all of your life, you are going to enjoy peace.

Now, since this book is about money and God's financial plan, we are going to look at that aspect of prosperity, so that we can know that God wants His kids to prosper. As we look at biblical prosperity, would that include debt? Of course not. Proverbs 22:7 and Romans 13:8 confirm that:

> *"...the borrower is slave to the lender."*

> *"Let no debt remain outstanding, except the continuing debt to love one another, for whoever loves others has fulfilled the law."*

Debt harms and destroys your hope and future. God doesn't want to harm us; He wants to give us hope and future. Debt is a tool of the devil to keep believers in bondage, so we are stressed and can't give into Kingdom work. God's financial plan doesn't include debt, however as we are growing in faith, we may need debt for a house or car. If we continue to pursue His plan, God will show us how to pay cash for everything, yes even a house.

So, clearly debt is not part of prosperity. Also, struggling paycheck to paycheck is not part of His plan. God is a God of abundance. There is no lack in God or His Kingdom and since you are a citizen of His Kingdom, there shouldn't be any lack in your life either. That includes your finances. Also, God doesn't want you to have just enough to pay the bills. He wants you to tithe (10%), give (whatever amount He puts on your heart, but generously), pay your bills, and have money left over to enjoy life and bless others. That's what it means to prosper in Jeremiah 29:11.

Because the enemy has done such a good job of destroying the word prosperity in the church, I feel the need to hammer this home. As a human father or mother, do you want your kids to be poor and in debt? Do you want them stressing over money and fighting about it in their marriage? Do you want them without food? A working car? Homeless? Of course not. You want them to be complete and not lacking in every area of life. So, why would be think that our heavenly Father would want His children to struggle financially? He doesn't, but the enemy does, so stop listening to the lies and fill your heart and mind with the truth of God's word. God has plans to prosper you. Believe it!

Okay, let's move on to debt elimination. Before we can talk about eliminating debt, we must talk about the dreaded B word – BUDGET. For many people budget is like a swear word. That may be, but it's a critical part of God's financial plan. He wants you to know what your financial picture looks like and the only way you can do that is a budget.

If you are a computer wizard and like accounting, you can use software or a phone/tablet app. If you are like my wife and I and want to keep it simple, you can just create a bill sheet that shows the amount of money coming in each month and a list of all the bills or spending categories. You can find those easily by looking at your bank account and credit card account. When we were deeply in debt, Karen and I used this system to have a visual for where we were spending money and it helped us determine places where we could cut expenditures. More on that later in this chapter.

As we talked about in chapter two, God expects us to be good stewards of the money He provides. A budget enables us to create a spending plan that ensures we will always have enough to tithe, give, cover our needs and some wants, and even save and invest. A budget helps us get out of debt and prepare for the future. We still use this same, simple budgeting system over two decades later and are still debt free (except for our mortgage and a car loan with no interest). God's ways work!

Just in case you are still thinking you can do this without a budget, here are eight benefits of budgeting:

1. You control your money rather than money controlling you.
2. Helps you stay focused on your money and life goals.
3. Keeps you consistently aware of your spending.
4. Helps you stay organized.
5. Forces you to decide in advance on spending.
6. Enables you to save.
7. Provides early warning of potential problems.
8. Helps you make decisions.

Hopefully you are seeing the reasons for having a budget. Everyone who is serious about getting and staying out of debt must have a budget. The important thing to know is that it doesn't have to be complicated, and you don't have to buy expensive software (you can if you want). As I mentioned earlier, Karen created what we call "The Bill Sheet". It's a simple Excel spreadsheet that lists our bills, the amount due each month, and when it's due. We plan our expenditures and giving based on that sheet and it has kept us on track and debt free for many years.

Obviously, if you have knowledge and want to use software, programs like QuickBooks are a great way to budget and track your expenses. If you have a business, this is a must and will help with your taxes.

After putting your budget in place, the next step in debt elimination is to cut from the budget:

- Stop using credit cards for six months to a year. Then you can begin using one card, as long as you pay it off weekly or monthly, that way there is never any accumulation or interest.
- Stop buying things that you can't afford and don't need. I am currently boycotting any company that sells items I can't afford or don't need and so should you.
- Make coffee at home instead of stopping by Starbucks, Dutch Bros, or your local

coffee shop – just $3 per day (and you probably spend more) is $90 per month. Later, I'll show you how you can quickly pay off debt using that extra money.

- Research and reduce your cell phone plan – do you actually need unlimited data. Check out all the major cell service companies and the others, such as Boost, Cricket, Mint, Consumer Cellular, and so on. Compare the plans, and find the one that is going to work best with your new budget.

- Research and reduce your television plan – we eliminated our expensive cable plan in favor of a window antenna and stayed that way until we got debt free. It gave us all the local channels and then later we added less expensive streaming services to get the other channels or movies we wanted.

- Research and reduce your internet plan – you may be able to get away with a slower speed or find a deal with another company.

- Reduce your entertainment. Find fun, free entertainment, such as museums, parks, hikes, board games, etc.

- Identify other costs you could reduce or eliminate.

- Also, if you're married, establish a dollar amount for purchases without speaking with your spouse. Many years ago, we established that amount at $50 and have stuck to it.

The next step to debt elimination is to add the savings from above to the money you are already paying toward debt. In this section, I will share with you what we did that enabled us to pay off $120,000 in consumer debt in just five years.

I'm writing this book is 2022 and U.S. citizens are carrying $856 billion in just credit card debt. That's an increase of $52 billion from $804 billion in the third quarter of 2021. Americans are in debt up to their eyeballs. It's an epidemic that must be stopped. Debt and money issues are typically one of the biggest problems mentioned in marriage counseling and often becomes a reason for divorce. Also, debt is dramatically impacting the ability to give, so it's slowing the growth of the Kingdom of God.

Start your debt elimination plan now. If you have any high interest credit cards or loan balances, see if you can balance transfer to a 0% interest card and then pay it off before the interest kicks in. You can check out cards on CreditCards.com and click on 0% APR, under Card Category, to find cards. Find the longest 0% period, again with the goal of paying off the balance before the end of the 0% interest term.

Also, it never hurts to call your current credit card or loan company to see if they will lower the rate. If you have multiple cards/loans, call the oldest first (as loyalty often counts). Make sure you are speaking with a supervisor or someone who has the authority to lower your interest rate. Don't take the first no. Keep saying that there must be a way to get your interest lowered. Mention the amount of time you've had the card and push your loyalty.

If you have enough self-control and will not use the cards, take them out of your wallet and put them somewhere safe and where you can't easily get them. A safety deposit box at your bank or credit union or a combination safe at home are preferred. If you don't have a safe and don't want to spend the extra money, put them in a box in your attic, basement or on a high shelf. The harder they are to get, the easier this will be. If you don't have enough self-control, cut the cards and keep them until you are ready to close the accounts.

Okay, now we are ready for the five-step debt elimination process:

1. Make a list of your debts from lowest balance to highest.

2. Total the balances, so you know what size mountain you are dealing with.

3. Prayer – place those bills on a table and begin speaking to the mountain. Mark 11:23, "I tell you the truth, you can say to this mountain, 'May you be lifted up and thrown into the sea,' and it will happen. But you must really believe it will happen and have no doubt in your heart."

4. Snowball – take the money you saved from the earlier step and apply it to the credit card or loan that has the lowest balance. Continue doing this, adding any extra money to this payment, until it is completely paid off. Take that entire payment and add it to the current payment on the next lowest credit card or loan balance. Pay it off and continue through your list until everything has been paid off. This would include any car loans.

5. Once you have paid off all the credit cards and loans, begin to add that total amount to your regular monthly mortgage payment to accelerate paying off your mortgage. If you don't have a mortgage, put the total amount into an account that earns interest. Build it up until you have the equivalent of at least two months' worth of your expenses. That will be your security fund, so you will never have to fall back into debt.

All the money that you save or extra money you receive (including tax returns) should be used to quickly pay down the debt. This is an aggressive debt elimination program that has worked for many people and it's the one we used to eliminate $120,000 in consumer debt in just 5 years. If you work it, it will work for you.

In the final chapter, we're going to look at how you can increase your income, so you can pay down that debt even quicker.

Chapter Seven: Activation

Personal Activities

1. If you don't already have a budget, create one.
2. Next, make a list of your expenses and figure out where you can cut costs – internet, TV, cell service, entertainment, coffee, etc. Cut as much as you can and then make a note of the amount you are saving.
3. Make a list of your debts from the lowest amount to the highest and begin paying what you saved in part 2, along with your normal payment. Pay that debt off and then move the entire amount to the next debt on your list. Work through the list until you are debt free.

Small Group Discussion Questions

1. Why doesn't God's financial plan include debt (other than necessary debt such as a mortgage, business, or car loan)?
2. The lesson talked about having a budget – do you have one? If not, why not?
3. What are some of the ways that you are going to use to cut debt?

Chapter Eight:
Financial Increase

In this final chapter, I'm going to share some ideas for increasing the amount of money that comes into your home, so you can pay the debt down even quicker. We used these to pay down the $120,000 debt and continue to use some of them as primary income sources, now that we are retired.

Part-Time Business -

So, a part-time business is one way to do that. Perhaps you have a skill that you could market – bookkeeping, recordkeeping, consulting, plumbing, construction, landscaping, pool maintenance, house cleaning or you could make items for sale. Most of these will enable you to start part-time and build up the income. The downside to many of these is that you will have to invest a lot of money into equipment, tools, systems, etc. The upside is that if you can get started and gain a couple of customers, you will have increased your income and can more quickly pay down your debt.

Network Marketing -

If you're like me and don't have any of those marketable skills, you could join a network marketing company. They are like franchises, except without all the fees. We've seen thousands of people generate great part-time and full-time incomes through network marketing. We generated a lot of extra money through network marketing, which we used to pay off our mountain of debt quicker. I even wrote books teaching people how to become successful in network marketing.

One of the biggest benefits of this type of business is that it's a turn-key business. The company has already developed the products or services, ordering and distribution systems, websites, etc. Plus, it has a very low entry investment and low operational costs, but the upside is unlimited. I know many people who started into network marketing deeply in debt and struggling to make ends meet. Now, they are debt free, quite well off and enjoying both time and financial free. Network marketing is not for everyone, but perhaps it will be your answer for increasing income.

If you're going to go this route, please feel free to consult with me, so I can give you some tips on finding the right company and sponsor. You can email me at Rod@RodNichols.com.

Internet Businesses -

The internet has opened many great part-time opportunities to increase income. You can learn how to build sales funnels and offer that as a business or use the **funnels** to sell products or services. I use a sales funnel to enroll students in my online Bible school, True Disciple Academy (trued700iscipleacademy.com). This funnel is built in Groove, but I have also used ClickFunnels in the past. I like that Groove is a multi-functional platform and would be happy to answer questions. Feel free to email me with questions. ClickFunnels is another good system to use to create landing pages and sales funnels.

Another great opportunity is **affiliate marketing**. There is a lot of great training available through ClickBank.com. On that site you will also find many affiliate opportunities. I used a couple of affiliate marketing programs to increase our income. It's pretty easy to add an additional $50 to $200 per month through affiliate marketing. One of my favorite financial testimonials was because of an affiliate program. I was consistently making $30 to $50 per month, which we were applying to our debt elimination plan. However, we had a month where there was an unexpected expense of $400. On the day this bill was due, we received a $400 payment through the affiliate program. It was by far the largest payment we ever received. Praise God!

Coaching -

Coaching is another rapidly growing home business opportunity. You could be a life coach, business coach, spiritual coach, physical fitness coach, weight loss coach, health coach. Think about what you are good at and could coach other people. Coaching sessions can be in person or via Zoom. You can charge by the hour and offer packages. I have an acquaintance who was deeply in debt and struggling with life. She invested in a coaching training and certification program and is now making as much as $10,000 per month.

Online Education -

A quickly expanding area is developing and marketing online courses. Do you have a particular knowledge or expertise that you could turn into an online course? You can shoot video using your iPhone or Android and upload into any number of course platforms. I'm using Groove to build my online courses. I've also extensively researched Thinkific, Teachable, Kajabi, and Kartra. Feel free to ask questions using the email I provided earlier in this lesson.

Part-Time Job -

You could secure a 2nd job and for a short season, work hard to generate enough extra income to get debt free, then quit the job. The key is to make sure this doesn't jeopardize your relationship with God, family, or the church.

Many people are now driving for Lyft or Uber and making very good money part-time. You dictate when you drive, so you can work it around a full-time job and family. Also, there are many companies looking for part-time delivery drivers. Go to Indeed.com and search for part-time driver.

Another good part-time job is working **customer service** from your home. You can find opportunities at https://www.ariseworkfromhome.com.

Education -

You could go back to school to gain new knowledge or degrees that would help you gain a promotion at your current job or find a better one.

When our business crashed in 2011, we began searching for ways to improve our financial future. Through the state and county governments (Arizona), both of us received grants for schooling – Karen in Microsoft Office and mine in web design. Karen's education allowed her to secure a job at Goodwill as a Career Advisor and mine helped me to secure a job with a new ministry.

Remember to use all increases in income to more quickly pay down the debt.

What You've Learned in This Book -

Let's do a quick recap of the book:

Mindset – God wants you to have a prosperous mindset. *Shalowm* – not lacking anything. Jesus had an abundance mentality, and He wants you to have that same mentality.

Stewardship – Everything belongs to God; He just lets us use His stuff. He does expect us to be good stewards of the talents, time, and money He gives us. The parable of the talents teaches us that production is not as important as action.

Partnership – It's so amazing that we have an invitation to partner with the Creator of the Universe! We are to partner with God, other Christians, and the church to fulfill God's plan on earth. When we partner with God, He will prosper us!

Sowing and Reaping – This is a law that God created from the very beginning. It works every time. The money God gives you is for food (costs of living) and sowing. If you don't sow, you will not reap. Those who sow generously, will reap generously.

Tithing – Everything belongs to God and our partnership is such that God provides all the capital and only asks for 10% of the increase. You get to keep the other 90%! Tithe = 10% of your gross income, bonuses, commissions, gifts, any money you receive that you haven't tithed on. Tithing carries two huge promises – overflowing blessings and protection for the rest of what God has given you.

Giving/Offerings – Giving or offerings is what you give above the tithe. God gave us this world and His Son, what are you willing to give back. He wants us to be cheerful and generous givers. He also wants us to test him and be sacrificial givers – give until it hurts and watch what God does. Lastly, He wants your first and best!

Let's end with a joke (author unknown):

A preacher got up one Sunday and announced to his congregation:

"I have good news and bad news…"

"The good news is, we have enough money to pay for our new building program!"

"The bad news is, it's still in your pockets!"

It's time to get out of debt and become cheerful, generous givers, so that we can grow the Kingdom of God here on earth!

CHAPTER EIGHT: ACTIVATION

Personal Activities

1. Evaluate the list of possible part-time businesses or if you have your own idea, begin the process of launching a business you can work part-time from home.

2. Evaluate your current job to see if there is some education you could seek, that would result in a promotion or increase in pay. See the Lord for whether this is a correct path and if it is, ask about the timing to start.

Small Group Discussion Questions

1. List some of the ways you can increase your finances that were discussed in this lesson.

2. Of those listed, which are appealing to you to increase your finances and get out of debt quicker?

3. Reviewing the recap of the course, what lessons impacted you most? What have you done during the course to change your financial situation?

OTHER BOOKS BY
ROD NICHOLS

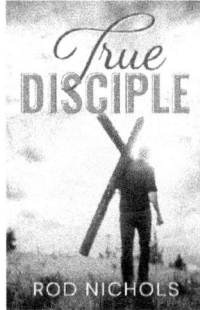

Throughout the Bible we find ordinary, fallible people just like us. These ordinary people did extraordinary things. Then along came Jesus. He said that his followers would do even greater things than he did. A mind-blowing promise! Yet, most believers haven't experienced the miracles we see in God's Word. What is the difference between the people in the Bible and those sitting in any of our churches?

The answer to that question is found in Rod Nichols' new book, True Disciple. Rod believes the Lord instructed him to write his true disciple story. He was (and still is) one of those ordinary, fallible people that God taught to be a true disciple of Jesus Christ. Rod is real and transparent about his struggles, doubts, fears, questions, and failures. He shares some amazing adventures and what he learned along the way. With God's help, these lessons could transform any ordinary person into a mountain moving true disciple.

In True Disciple, Nichols hopes to motivate the church to love God with all they have and to love people as Jesus loved us; to get out from those comfy seats and secure walls and go do what Jesus commanded - preach the gospel to the world, make disciples, heal, deliver, and help those in need. Are you ready for the adventure of a lifetime? Would you like to have God use you to change the world around you? True Disciple will prepare you for an amazing journey!

**Order at www.TrueDisciple.Info
or on Amazon and other online retailers.**

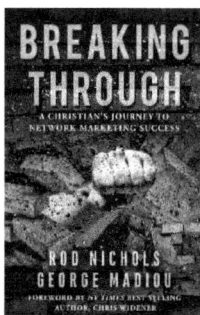

Tim is a struggling network marketer. His wife is hounding him to quit. His friends think he's crazy and avoid him at social gatherings. He's frustrated and ready to surrender but decides to give his business one last chance at a company convention in Hawaii. There he hopes to find the magic answers to success and the life of his dreams. A surprise encounter changes Tim's life and unveils the true secrets to network marketing success.

Successful network marketing veterans, Rod Nichols and George Madiou have crafted a fun to read story with engaging characters. This book is packed with real world business building secrets that could change your life and the trajectory of your network marketing business. If you can relate to Tim, Breaking Through is a must read.

Order on Amazon and other online retailers

Contact Rod Nichols: Rod@RodNichols.com